Life is a Challenge
Not a Pass

An Autobiography

bill martin vivatson

Binford & Mort Publishing
Portland, Oregon

Dedication

This autobiography is a living legacy that "No man is an island unto himself." It chronicles scores of incidents where strangers encouraged the author through trials, challenges, success and adventure.

To my wife, the one who trusted and shared my many dreams, it was her faith and patience that made all things possible.

To my friends and mentors Al and Ceil Podell and to the one who inspired the writing of this journal, Lorraine Sohm.

Cover Art: Robert J. Hildebrand
Photo Restoration: John Wardlaw
Illustrations: Laura Vivatson

Life is a Challenge, Not a Pass

Printed in the United States of America

Library of Congress Catalog Card Number: 2006927858

ISBN: 0-8323-0563-4 pbk
ISBN: 0-8323-0562-6
First Edition 2006

Contents

Acknowledgement

Marriage defined by experts:

According to the Apostle Paul, it is a guarantee of trouble.

And, geniuses like Einstein offered this, "It is mans effort to make something last out of an incident."

But for me, it was a stage where my future would be shared.

If one word would describe my wife, it is "steadfast". If one word described her weakness, it was "reckless". For she chose a mate whose dreams of bricks, mortar and far away places were those of a man who had no future to share.

Along with her, I inherited a new family who welcomed me. With her mother Claire, I soon enjoyed "favorite son" status and she was my hero. There was also her sister Kay and aunties Kate, Bessie and Florine.

She was a wife without agenda of her own, but it was us, me, Laura and Claire, who she served with zeal and purpose. With bills, payments and not enough cash, she honed her skills as a master of finance. In her house no one ever went without.

Then one day, as if by plan, she made it possible for her clan to move across the tracks where opportunity was waiting. It became a place where doors were opened to us as if angels paved the path. Across the tracks there were people waiting for me with names like Podell, Barlow, Zuravin, Stephenson, Armstrong, Biedebach, Maitland and Sakaroff. It was a stage for a lowly farm boy who would finally behold that by his hands his dreams would unfold. For one who never could measure his worth, it was by grace that others would. Even so, the dreams of prosperity are an illusive game that when given by the Master it can come with a price. It was like a whirlwind, her family's fortunes flourished, but one day soon the doors would close.

In a grand finale, the Great One must have said to this kid of the prairie, I will grant his boyhood dream of sailing a tropical sea. The gift was a ketch I called *Still Waters* and on June 1, 1977 it carried me to Hawaii where my family would join me soon. It was a summer when time stood still and her family celebrated, how good was the gift of life. Very often many asked, "Weren't you afraid on that great ocean?" I always answered no, and added, "What I have is not mine to lose."

It was Christmas of 1977 when we were invited to celebrate the completion of the Sakaroffs' new home by the sea. The lavish setting was for those of means and an unlikely place for a farm boy to be seen. Servants were dressed in black and white, elegant drinks and food were the fare of the night. I was stopped by the door by a royal audience who asked, "Is this your creation?" It was as though with great relief that I would answer with truth from where it all came. He coached my words to sing the praises of my gift as an architect that He alone had made. That night I lived His words of record that read, "Show me a man skilled with his hands and I will show you a man who will stand before kings." Yes, she too shared that night and as we left a quiet voice told us, "It is enough." It was my grand finale.

As pen and paper were put away and hammer and saws fell silent, we moved on to a new stage of adventure, challenge and purpose. It is for this reason we can celebrate 28 years in Kona.

For too many, the magic of a 50th marriage anniversary is but a trophy, however for us it has been the blessed adventure of trying to follow the footsteps of the One who ordains all things.

Perhaps she said it best, as if prophetic, at our Christmas party in 1963 when we celebrated our move across the tracks. With Tom at the keyboard, how beautifully she sang a song called, "Bill." The "Bill" she sang about was plain, ordinary me. He was hardly a candidate for such a life of privilege.

Since that night of 42 years ago I can proudly say, I would trade my life with no man.

bill martin vivatson
50th Wedding Anniversary Tribute

CHAPTER ONE

My Beginning

Where a story begins is never as important as its ending. For me, my beginning was in total contradiction to the final chapters I am living today.

I was born on 6 June 1925 in a little house on a very small farm in Pembina County, North Dakota, close to a little village called Halson, a place that has disappeared from the road maps decades ago.

If I remember right I arrived on earth only five years after the state of North Dakota initiated the issuance of the first birth certificate. When my birth certificate was filled out there was either a big family argument or a moment of indecisiveness. Mine reads as follows;

Name. Baby Boy Vivatson (name lined out)
        Vilhjalmar Vivatson (name lined out)
        William Martin Vivatson

Martin Johnson, my namesake and grandfather who lost his farm during the Great Depression, sister Gloria, age 6 and author, age 11.

My Beginning

Pembina County was the most northeasterly place in the state. On the west side of the county was the village of Halson, a place of poor land where the farm families struggled to make it produce a living. As a child I was well aware of poverty but I always lived with the confidence that my parents could provide for us four children. They were a great example to me.

However, I had two life long handicaps, one I was born with and the other I acquired. In spite of these handicaps I would be able to achieve a successful career, fulfill all my childhood dreams, and retire at age 51! This journal is written to point the way for others to become achievers.

Seventy five years after my birth, the year 2,000 census was taken. It is now three years later and the statistics that are being revealed are frightening. The once independent and resourceful people who settled the nation have produced a new generation of those who cannot care for themselves. And all these dependent people will never know a success in their lifetime.

Here are some statistics of failure; — 80 % of our elderly are poor; — 35 % depend totally on our welfare programs to survive; — 70 % live from paycheck to paycheck; — the average household credit card debt is $8,000; — 80 % of all baby boomers will enter retirement with huge house payments; — and the worst statistic of all is that only 10% of all tax payers pay 70 % of all taxes. I have to ask, what happened, have we become a nation of free loaders?

I want my story to be a challenge to those who have given up and to those who might say, "I don't have a chance."

Success in life can be an elusive goal. For those born into wealth it will only be a challenge of treading water. Meaning, don't lose what you have. But for the rest of us, our success is usually in the hands of others. It will be other people who will recognize our talents and potential. It is their money that will pay us for our worth. In other words, our success is not a solitary accomplishment.

I would like to introduce you to the people who counted in my life, who taught me to do things right and be responsible, and took the time to mold my life in a way my busy parents never could.

Perhaps you picked up this journal because of the title. If you did I trust you will find information and basic truths that will permit you to achieve success. The word 'success' in the original ancient languages

3

meant, 'to be complete'. I am seldom impressed with our weekly news slicks that attempt to establish who is successful. True success is far more illusive than their simplistic standards.

Success in life can only follow our desire to develop initiative. If you feel you lack this virtue practice will do wonders. Initiative is simply the practice of being totally involved with everything that impacts your life.

I invite you to come with me and meet the first people who gave direction to my inherent initiative. They were not giants but they possessed all the standards for being great role models.

I was in the third grade when Mr. Shultz came into my life. He was hired to bring order and discipline to a flagging school district that was being run over by overgrown bad boys. He would replace Miss Tisdale who no longer could control this gang. After a few days Mr. Shultz was in control, the bad boys lost and he remained there for the next six years. To this day, I feel he was there for me.

All eight grades shared the small one room school. On average about 35 farm children attended. All were poor. The Spartan structure had the basic old fashioned desks with ink wells. In the front of the room were the teacher's desk and two wooden benches where the kids were called up for class time. On the front wall was a pull down world map and a world globe suspended from the ceiling with cord and pulleys. On a table was a four inch thick dictionary. This was North Dakota Public Education.

My first attachment to this teacher was because of his personality of authority. He spoke with conviction in what he believed. As each class was called forward to the benches, the rest of the students were expected to be quiet and do their homework.

My problem was I wanted to hear everything the seventh and eighth grade kids were learning. One day, the first time for me, he pulled down the globe from the ceiling. I watched intently from my desk as he described to the class where the equator was, what the latitudes and longitudes are, the track of the earth around the sun and why we have winter and summer. When he spoke of the continents and countries I was all ears. Never once did Mr. Shultz scold me to get busy on my homework. But how interesting is the coincidence that all those things I would learn about the globe would one day be a crucial part of a grand adventure later in life. Everything he said I believed and absorbed.

4

My Beginning

About the year I was in fifth grade I remember Mr. Shultz arriving at school one morning with two sheets of plywood. This was a big day for a school that had nothing. As he untied the pieces of plywood he asked us boys to carry them down to the school basement. He continued to unload bags of new tools, nails, glue, sand paper and paint. He had paid for everything. That day in school he announced that at recess and lunch hour he would help us build small projects we could take home with us. The first day all the boys were anxious to be part of learning wood work.

First we would learn how to use the hand tools. (Of course there was no electricity.) He showed us how to saw a straight line, how to use the plane and assemble the pieces of wood. It was not long before the other kids were out playing and Mr. Shultz and I were left to turn these two sheets of plywood into magazine racks, shelves and book ends.

Today I am old and there is a word I now seldom use, that is the word, 'coincidence'. Instead, I believe that the very day Mr. Shultz brought the plywood and tools to school was a prophetic introduction to the direction of my life. These symbolic boards and tools would be the things my talent and career were built on. Mr. Shultz was a generous man.

The second role model to cross my path was Mr. Christopherson, my high school principal. He was a tall portly man, always well dressed in suit and bow tie, full of confidence and well equipped for teaching discipline and the basics, like math. He was not to be carelessly ignored.

In 1940 in my second year of high school the school introduced a new optional class, 'shop'. Although we had electricity the only power tool our new shop had was a small grinder; all else were basic hand tools. The new teacher would be Mr. Mutz, who was now teaching math as well as biology.

Mr. Mutz was the third role model in my young life. He shared the character traits of the other two. He was devoted to and serious about his work. He was not a tall man like our principal but there was an aura of authority in his actions and words. He was always well dressed and well mannered. All his students respected him simply for the way he spoke to us; our questions were answered as though we were the only person in class.

He was a man of facts and figures who convinced me that is what I wanted to be, not a teacher but knowledgeable. Once again I would be one of the few young men who had much interest in shop. It was optional with little credit and few takers. Soon it would be Mr. Mutz and I building things like bookcases and display boards for the class-rooms. And I did absorb all he taught me about the use and application of tools. Of course these were simple beginnings, but as I look back they were building blocks I yet did not understand. After just one year Mr. Mutz was called away to the war and I never heard about him again.

It was fall of 1940 and my third year in high school. There would be no Mr. Mutz and the school shop was locked for the duration of the war. I was very disappointed.

One day our principal Mr. Christopherson called me to his of-fice. With few words he handed me a key to the shop and told me that Miss Wagner, out English teacher and head of faculty, had some projects she needed. He told me I was not to permit any students in the shop. I never did. Like an afterthought he added, "William, you can keep the key." I was certain that Mr. Mutz was responsible for recommending me.

Miss Rosie Wagner was a stately woman who exuded class and authority. She was tall and well dressed. I was possibly her worst student because I had little interest in English, much less literature. But she always seemed to overlook my deficiencies and addressed my shortcomings with a typical comment like, "Oh William, I know you can do better."

In my senior year she wisely demanded every student to read one book every two months, complete with book report. It was a demand-ing task for someone into projects. I learned how to fake a book report by reading the introduction flap and by reading opening paragraphs of a few chapters. But during the later half of my senior year Miss Wagner singled me out and informed me that she was wise to my inadequate book reports. She said that I was to check out a book from the library and I was to read it from cover to cover. I was to write the report and present it with the book for her review. I had been outsmarted.

I went to the library and took time to find something I really wanted to read since it had to be a whole book. My choice was an autobiogra-phy called, *The World At My Fingertips*. It was a story about a younger man who was a writer and journalist who had acquired an irreversible eye disease that would eventually make him permanently blind. The story was a day by day venture into the world of darkness and his ability to cope with his affliction. His new adventure in life would be lived through his typewriter and his skill to use it. I read it from cover to cover with great interest. Miss Wagner, for once, was pleased with me. How prophetic my book choice would turn out to be! In less than five years, my life would be turned up side down with my own crisis of blindness.... Would Miss Wagner's demands of me be a preparation for things to come?

I do not want to leave anyone with the idea that my recipe for success is cast in stone. It is simply what worked for me. However, there are basic principles of human conduct that permitted my success to happen. Today we live in a time where young adults want a leg up to assure their success. It might be a student loan, a new car as reward for being a good student or plenty of free time to chase a ball around a court or field just so he can feel good about himself.

Success is an illusive target. It has many meanings to us. But I have my own opinion and that is; Success is a personal achievement well planned and executed so that it is possible to pass it on to others, who can benefit from it. It has been a humbling experience.

There was an incident midpoint in my career that describes this best. I had completed a set of preliminary drawings for an oceanfront home. I called the clients to pick up the plans for their review. When they came to get them the gentleman stopped for a moment and said, "Bill, you haven't even asked us for a retainer and now you are simply giving me the plans. What if we took them to someone else?" My answer was, "That's all right because I have the recipe."

My recipe is this; The root of success will nearly always start in the work place or the market place. Both are constantly on the lookout for special people. Special people, I have found, share these four attributes; *Curiosity – Enthusiasm – Memory – and Energy.* I would like to attempt to explain each and pretend you are at your place of work:

Curiosity. Webster; 'a desire to know."
- Be constantly aware of your surroundings.
- Be interested in what your employer is trying to do.
- Never be afraid to ask questions.
- Know everything about your job and product.
- Think of how you could improve your job.

Enthusiasm. Webster; "eager interest."
- It is something you give away when you use it.
- It is contagious.
- It sets you apart as special.
- You don't worry that your boss is making money from your ideas and effort.
- You will be noticed.

Memory. Webster; "power or act to remember'.
- It is the basic measure of I.Q.
- Employers want smart people.
- It is something that can be developed.
- The ability to remember is a sign of a good employee.
- It is where the treasures of life are stored.
- Memory thrives on important things like facts and figures. Not fleeting simple things like sports and play.

Energy. Webster; vigor, power, capacity to do work.
- It is the simple act of getting up in the morning and doing something, anything productive.
- It is the desire to keep busy and be productive.
- Energy grows from worthwhile things.

It is possible that these are simplistic ideas but I can assure you that if you apply them, your self-worth will take a new direction. As a poor farm boy I could bring few things to the table of opportunity. Essentially nothing. But my energy propelled me to celebrate many wonderful experiences of life like; hiking the John Muir trail from Lake Tahoe to the top of Mt. Whitney. — In the past 11 years traveling solo by bicycle 8,500 miles in Western Europe. — Working as a volunteer in refugee camps in far away places that would increase the size of our family. Energy, the magic of life itself.

So come with me and meet these wonderful people who sensed these qualities in a simple young man and said, 'Let's give him a hand.'

By May of 1943 I would have little to look forward to other than a call from the draft board. For the next four years my life would come under the heavy hand of others. But even so, there would be those who gave unexpected direction and purpose to my life. Come meet the people whose generous acts enriched my life and impacted its direction.

CHAPTER TWO

Life on the Prairie with Once Strong People

North Dakota. The first sight stirs negative emotions that vary from bad weather to the appearance of an eternal void. And for 50 years or more I agreed with them. But if I must claim this as my birthplace I certainly have something to remember. Life in Pembina County in the 1920s was a challenge of survival on a daily basis. I left the place before my 18th birthday and always bragged, "I never looked back." Fortunately today I have a different story to tell because it is said, 'pain has no memory' and we all take something valuable from even a difficult past.

If we look at the past seven decades of social change in America it is easy for me to say, the achievement and heritage of the noble people of the prairie have no equal. Today America can only boast statistics of failure that makes one wonder what civilization is all about. The people of the prairie had four core values that made them giants of their time. They were; 1. Conscience, sense of right or wrong. 2. Character, moral strength. 3. Responsibility, obligation to do. 4. Fear, anticipation of danger. It would be in January 1932 that a new era would spell the end to these noble human traits. Within one decade the seeds of Socialism were well planted. As a child I would witness the best man could do and also live to see him at his worst.

Today the state of North Dakota, on a per capita basis, is one of the highest consumers of national welfare, food stamps and housing subsidies. Since 1940 there are few farm states that have learned to manipulate farm subsidies as they have. My own parents, once hardened prairie survivors, by 1945 had found themselves entrapped by the promises of federal farm subsidies. It is said of the North Dakota farmer, — "If you want to double your income simply put up two mail boxes!"

This chapter is to bring honor to a people of the prairie who have long ago vanished as teachers and examples of excellence and independence. These people are my heroes and their examples made my life full and rich. I dedicate this chapter to them. I lived their poverty and I was better for it. I witnessed their pain of trial and it would later strengthen me. The prairie, like life, is a magical place of regeneration. Although it may die in autumn it is the rebirth of spring where it expresses itself best. And it does it again and again. And I liken my life to it, so many chances, so many opportunities and so many blessings. Come with me and let us pretend it is spring.

The Red River Valley was once an ancient lake. As the water drained away it left untold square miles of wet lands and shallow waterways. If there was an ice box version of the Garden of Eden, this was it. These low lying waterways were a natural habitat of migratory birds and also a place of bountiful varieties of wild fruit bearing trees and shrubs. These were so prolific in season that there were many winters that the only preserved fruit we had or could afford was wild. The prairie abounded with millions of edible wildlife like prairie chicken, pheasant, partridge and jack rabbit. Any farmer had only to dig a hole in the soft soil about ten feet deep and have pure well water in abundance. And in spring and summer the plains rolled with wild flowers and song birds. Only nature fills the void of a prairie best.

The prairie floor was strewn with broken arrow heads and sculptured stone clubs which revealed others were here before the settlers. When I was a child I can remember old people who would tell stories about sharing the prairie with the Indians.

As I reflect about my childhood I know I had a passion for the natural beauty that surrounded my simple life. From early spring to the killing frost of autumn I knew everything that nature had to offer. I knew all the birds and where they nested. As the season progressed I knew where all the wild fruit could be found. The deep water holes of the coulees were my favorite haunts. It was the only place to swim, yet I would be the generation that would witness the eventual destruction of the prairie. By 1960 the modern farmer had destroyed the prairie. Today every square acre of grass land, — every creek or coulee has been drained or filled — every rose bush or tree and even wild fruit or berry tree has been destroyed by bulldozers. And whatever else the modern farmer considered his natural enemy was destroyed with chemicals or a rifle. So devastating was the cost of progress that eventually clean water had to be piped into Pembina County.

In the past decade the city of Grand Forks would be destroyed by a flood of epic proportions. It was caused by destruction of the water shed by farmers. Today the people of the Red River Valley are a poor people.

When I arrived in Pembina County my father was a musician by natural talent, education and temperament. When he and my mother were married they had the luxury of living with his parents until their second child was born. Their welcome had worn thin and the fortunes of a musician had gone bad and he had to become a farmer. The farm, a gift to mother by uncle Hans, was 80 acres of marginal land. Their first home was a 12 x 20-foot one room school house that had outgrown its' space. It became a granary and later a horse barn. My father had little talent as a carpenter and any improvements he attempted only made the place appear worse. I can honestly say we had about the shabbiest farm in the county. Only the hill people in the brush land fared worse.

What is primitive? For starters let us try no electricity, no phone, no running water and the toilet 50 feet from the house. The only available fuel for heat and cooking was scrub wood. In summer the refrigerator was the cellar floor and in winter the whole state was one.

For most of my childhood we only had kerosene wick lamps. It was a little better than a candle. Laundry was done with tub and board. I can never remember seeing any new furniture come into our home. Anything that was added to the house came from a farm auction of some poor farmer who chose to throw in the towel. Nothing matched, every pot, utensils, plate or cup was different. Bedding and linens were a catch all from who knows where, even cotton flour bags sewn together. But the important thing was that there were enough multiple layers of bedding in the winter. Clothing was hand-me-downs and no two socks matched. There was no embarrassment for such deficiencies because everyone was in the same fix. One winter, in the depths of the depression, I went to school with one black shoe and one brown shoe and both for the same foot. The soles were held in place by wire.

Of all human traits, memory is the one I marvel most. Even in old age I find myself recalling detailed incidents of long ago. One such occasion was when my grandparents lost their farm in late fall of 1929. My grandparents were once wealthy people who lost everything to the bank. There was a large gathering at their home to bid them good-bye. There were so many people there that I remember us children playing in the stairway to the second floor. What I remembered best were the emotional farewells at the end of the evening. Perhaps it was a lesson on finances that would stick with me throughout my life.

In my young years I absorbed the hardships of my parents trying to survive on this marginal 80 acres. Survival was a serious business. Back then the little family farm looked like a mini Noah's Ark. We had to keep a variety of animals that would be for work, transportation, for food and to sell. The field crops were a variety of necessity and the family garden was no hobby. I well remember my mother had the best garden.

One of the great fears of the prairie people was severe illness or accident. The doctor was 13 miles away and a hospital was 50 miles away and no one had any money. A trip to or visit from a doctor was for life threatening reasons. A simple ache or pain was managed by home remedies. A tooth ache was no reason to see a dentist. You were given a clove stick to chew on for relief, and eventually the tooth would rot away.

The geography of the Red River Valley of the north made it a formidable place for survival. Geologists suggest that in ancient times huge deep ice fields of the glacial age caused the land mass to drop much like what occurred under the Greenland icecap. This long and very low valley is a spillway for the frigid arctic air to roll into the plains of Dakota and states beyond. Fierce blizzards could last for days. I have seen snow trapped in headlands that reached 12 feet high. For days nothing could move. The care and feeding of the farm animals was a difficult task that had to be done. Keeping warm in shacks without insulation was accomplished by constantly feeding wood burning stoves, all winter long.

To survive a North Dakota winter was to look forward to the experience of the orchestrated miracle of spring. It is a glorious event that can be best seen from the eyes of a curious child. To the well tested prairie farmer spring would mean only one thing, about five months of never ending work. It was not easy for the farmer to make his land produce all the things he would need for another winter. And he knew that the beauty of spring and summer also brings the ravaging bugs, the dust storms and cloud burst storms that will drive everything flat to the ground.

Where we lived near the Canadian border, summer is only 90 days long. It is recognized as a short time on the prairie that has no killing frost. The first nod of spring can have several false starts that can bring a late snow storm. The most reliable arrival of spring will be the haunting sounds of high flying honking geese heading into Canada. As the ground clears of snow the red breasted Robin is one of the first to arrive and spring is here.

It seemed to bring a schedule that kept the farmer busy well into fall. The fast moving season wouldn't tolerate a lazy farmer. Everything he planted had to be done by a certain time to assure a successful crop. And the ripening of each crop demanded just as much attention. The last late crop to be harvested was the all important potato, something that was on the table every day and we always planted enough to sell. By the time the potato harvest was over the killing frost would be turning the green leaves to brown and send them tumbling to earth. Then, as timed by a slow drum beat, the passing of each day would bring another winter ever closer to the prairie.

Dependable transportation on the prairie when I arrived was horse and buggy in the summer and horse and sleigh in the winter. The first car I remember was a Model T Ford with only one door on the right and it was cranked to start. Next to survival the farmer, like everyone else, would forsake everything for his wheels.

As I grew up on the farm the car was the only thing that made us feel civilized. It gave us social status as well as mobility to enjoy the simple things in life like spending Saturday evening in Cavalier. For the farmer there were two great social events that marked our summers. They were the celebration of 4th of July with a picnic in Walhala and the Pembina County Fair in late August. The farm people were very sociable and visiting the neighbors in the evening was great fun for us kids. You would never receive company without serving them something to eat.

What I remember best about the prairie was the strength and confidence these people exhibited. There were no whining farmers. All knew how to live with challenges and problems.

But January of 1932 would usher in an era that would soon destroy the resolve of the most self-reliant people that our nation ever had. It would be the advent of the arrival of Franklin and Elenore Roosevelt. Both were born, the pampered rich, and both embraced the promises of Socialism. At that time the Communist movement was very strong in the northeastern states. Their newspaper, *The Daily Worker* would even reach the mailbox on the farm.

Their promises of easy solutions reached across the nation and a foolish people, all quitters, joined the 'call for change'. New programs tumbled forth from Washington D.C. with catchy three letter logos that were intended to cure all of our problems. The CCC work projects were for the young men and the WPA was to make-work for the older men. It would be the first national program in American history that invented the saying. "Just Look Busy". This new Socialism was called, "The New Deal".

In 1934 I was a witness to one of the most hideous scenes of my childhood that was stamped on my mind forever. It went like this; One day in the barnyard, my father dug large and deep holes with a horse drawn earth shovel. The next day a large black sedan drove into the yard and two men dressed in suits emerged. They talked to my father a few minutes and returned to the sedan and retrieved two large rifles. My father ordered me to go in the house. I started in that direction but found a spot where I could get a better look. Soon my father started bringing out cattle from the barn and tied them to posts near the newly dug holes. Loud cracks resounded as the animals were shot. The men moved to the hog pens and again there

were shots. When the killing stopped my father pulled the animals into the holes with a horse and covered them with soil. I later learned that the purpose of this slaughter was to eliminate the overproduction of farm animals in order to drive up prices. My father was paid about five dollars for each animal shot. For the rest of my life this act represented the legacy of the Roosevelts.

There was little that would change for the farmer very soon. The great drought and dust storms of the prairie land of America were subsiding. A wetter cycle swept the land and there was a little improvement in the crops. But overall it was still wide spread poverty.

As remote as we were, there was always something to look forward to, or unexpected events that made us know someone knew we were here.

There were entrepreneurs who traveled the farm community peddling their wares. One time a group of cowboys came with dozens of wild horses bridled together offering them for sale. My father bought two of these wild beasts and they were never any good. Then there was the Watkins man who traveled from farm to farm in his old car selling spices and extracts like vanilla and maple. These were resourceful people who survived by their own determination and strength. There was no such thing as a government hand out to help them.

There were two resourceful merchants who impressed me when I was a child. They were young men who traveled around the farm community in a green covered wagon pulled by two horses. Their wagon contained what were called 'dry-goods' in that era. They sold work clothes like shirts, overalls, shoes, gloves and what ever the farm worker needed. In the wagon was a small living quarters for the two young merchants who spent the summer supplying the farmers.

This wagon was owned by the Mandel Department Store in Grand Forks, 80 miles away. In the spring they shipped by train the wagon, merchandise, horses and their two sons to the farm community. Whenever they showed up at the farm I was excited to see everything they offered. Not so with my father. Americans have a long history of bigotry and my father was no different. Whenever the wagon arrived my father would comment, "There come the damn Jews." I could not understand his statement and would resent it. It would be decades later that I came to know the reasons and why I was right.

There was one summer merchant we all looked forward to. That was the fish truck. He brought a variety of fish from the lake area of Minnesota. But later in the 1930s there was an odious merchant that hit the farms buying every kind of scrap metal the farmers were willing to sell. This scrap metal drive took place about 1938 and it was much later we learned it had all gone to Japan for their pending war effort.

Life is like an escape wheel of an old clock. There is but one direction and surely it makes the hands, like life, move ever forward. By 1940 the farm family life was improving. His once worthless farm products now found a market from the demands of wars an ocean away, like Europe. There was money for some of the good things of life like batteries for the radio so we could listen to Jack Benny, Edgar Bergan and Charlie, Amos and Andy and the sobering news of another battle cry. By now my father had his second tractor. There was still no electricity but everyday life was better. And one of the long awaited events was the remodeling of our old shack. It took some doing after it suffered the remodeling attempts of my father. But the Nelson brothers somehow used the old schoolhouse as a core and built more space around it. The finished job got a coat of paint, the first coat in perhaps 35 years.

By 1939 the storm clouds or war were gathering over Europe and the Germans were on the march again. Very quickly England would be the final front and America had no choice but to support her. The saber rattle of a primitive country called Japan was becoming a threat to the entire Pacific. On the coast, war plants like Boeing and Douglas were hiring new workers. The shipyards and foundries became busy and America began to prosper.

A new migration of people would leave the land and head for the two oceans and a new future. And the Roosevelts would have no victory, for it was the dynamics of WWII that ended the Great Depression.

December 7, 1941 changed everything. It would be less than 20 months until I left the farm. It would also ring down an end to the primitive life style of the farm community, forever. Young men would leave the farms for good. It would take four full years and millions of lives before these two angry and cruel nations were driven to destruction.

My last two years in high school were a time to develop my skills with my hands in the high school shop. All made possible by Mr. Christopherson.

About May 20, 1943 I would leave by bus from Cavalier and would travel to Michigan to visit my sister Lorraine. The selective service, draft, was serious business at that time. I would first have to register with the local draft board and when I reached Michigan I had to register again. However I had other plans. Like most boys I had the bug for airplanes and if I had my choice I would pick the air force. But the pace of the foot war was increasing because of the impending invasion of Europe. They curtailed air force enlistments and I wasn't excited about being a soldier. I had more of an attraction to the Pacific ocean, than marching, so I found out the closest U.S. Merchant Marine enlistment center was Minneapolis. My plan was to stop in Minneapolis and enlist. Every service man was given one month to take care of affairs before reporting.

The last few days before leaving were to gather my few belongings and my birth certificate with all it's scratched out names. I got a cheap suitcase and was ready. On a bright May morning my mother was ready to drive me to the Cavalier bus station. There was no one to say good-bye, they were all busy in the fields. I was feeling, "Is this all there is?"

I remember well that the emptiness of that moment left deep scars on my self-worth and feelings of no longer belonging. It is only natural and a ritual we all must pass.

For me, many years later, this moment would be a reference point to mark my journey of life. And it has been a life filled with opportunities, challenges, rewards and adventures far beyond my wildest boyhood dreams. That very day there would be thousands of young men like me leaving home. Like me they would be facing the demands of conscription, and unlike me, thousands would lose their lives in strange lands, deprived of a seat at the table of life.

This would be my first ride on a bus and soon I was more interested in this machine than the fact I was leaving home. The only thing disappointing was how slowly it traveled. By this time America was in a shortage crisis of everything including gasoline and tires. Their solution to alleviate the problem was to make every vehicle that rode on tires travel a maximum of 35 miles an hour. I would travel south to Grand Forks and then to Fargo, a distance of only 175 miles, but with all the stops it would be late evening when I arrived in Fargo. Hours later I would catch my bus to Minneapolis, packed with service men on the move. Now, I could feel the war.

It was far past midnight when we approached Minneapolis. The bus station was downtown but the place looked too dark and strange. I decided to wait in the bus station until daylight.

It would be the first time I stayed in a hotel. What luxury! The room had too many towels and a bathroom. I had slept on the bus so I decided to locate the Merchant Marine office. To my surprise it was in the heart of town and in a hotel. I made my way up to the floor where they were located. Until that day I had never been on an elevator and this would make my third ride. When I went in they asked for my birth certificate and draft board card. I filled in a few papers and turned them in to the uniformed man at the desk. When you are only 18 there is not much to write down.

This would be my first initiation to waiting on things of the military. There are times like this that I wish I remembered what I was feeling. All I could remember was the big posters around the room selling the service and the demands of a world war. Soon it was my turn and this would be my first physical examination. I didn't know what to expect. I thought things took too long. But I remember very well being sent to another room where a man with a pan of warm water and a syringe said he had to wash my ears to check my eardrums. I just found out why mothers keep telling their boys to wash their ears. Shortly another man came in and told him to stop. They handed me a towel and pointed to the doctor's room.

He was a kindly sort and asked me questions about my childhood health record. I didn't know of anything but he would run by me names of things I never heard of. The only one I remembered was the word, rheumatic fever. Then he said I have a severe irregular heart beat and that they can't take me. He told me to be sure to see a doctor.

It would not be for another 15 years until I knew that my erratic heart beat had a name, it was Arrhythmia. It is a genetic condition that causes the heart to lose rhythm and cause spasms. There is no cure and it became my lifetime companion. It would be a lifelong reminder of my mortality.

I spent the day walking around this wonderful big city. I went to a place to eat where you could walk along a big line and pick whatever you wanted. It was called The Forum Cafeteria. I even went to a large theater and this one wasn't made out of wood like the Roxy Theater in Cavalier. The bed felt good that night and the next day I left for Chicago.

The trip to Chicago was beautifully dressed in the color of spring. All the towns along the way looked like a place I would have chosen to live. However, the arrival in Chicago was something I was not prepared for. Everything was smoke black with screeching streetcar wheels coming at you from every direction. The bus station was like something in a war zone. I had an anxious wait until I left for Muskegon.

Afternote:

With purpose and reverence I have sung the praises of my roots. They were a people for whom I would never again find a match. The broad reach of their example provoked understanding of things as simple as patriotism for a country that gave them life, strength and opportunity. I recently found an old newspaper article that supported my regard for the prairie people. It was this; "North Dakotans bought $397 million worth of bonds in WWII — the most per person in the nation."

My next return to my home would be under circumstances I could never have imagined, and for which I had little preparation.

CHAPTER THREE
Growing Up in Michigan

The Chicago Greyhound bus station was in a tough neighborhood and I was happy to be on the way to Muskegon. It was the first time I had seen what an industrial city looked like. The narrow roadways were lined with factories for miles. I did not like what I saw; I could not help thinking about the people who had to work in these dreary places.

When I reached Michigan there were miles of farm land. I was on a local bus and it stopped at every village. The towns were very clean and prosperous. Every coffee or rest stop I looked forward to getting out and taking a look. How poor North Dakota seemed!

It was a slow trip to Muskegan. It was a commercial port town for grain freighters and passenger ferries. The terrain was nearly flat with sandy soil that produced only low scrub trees. There was little protection from the continuous winds that blew off Lake Michigan.

The old industrial town fronted the wharf where cargo ships as well as several large factories stood. Old brick buildings lined streets that radiated away from the town center. It looked more interesting than Cavalier. It was evident that this town, like many others, had fallen victim to the depression.

My sister Lorraine and her husband lived about 10 miles out of town where there was no bus service. My first order of business was to register with the Michigan draft board and then I looked for a job. They were for the asking. I immediately got a job in a new and very large factory that built radial aircraft engines for Pratt and Whitney. Eight hours a day and seven days a week, hours that were standard for most war plants.

This war brought with it many social changes that would never be reversed. An enigma of the defense plant towns was the loss of friendly and neighborly people. They became towns of strangers where few knew each other. In order to be closer to work and transportation, I rented a room from a wonderful elderly couple, Mr. and Mrs. Geyser. My sister had introduced me to her neighbor Al, who owned the town pool hall. Back then it was one of the few places for young men to hang out. He served light lunches and I found it good place to spend time in a lonely town. Al became my friend and he was a good source for learning all about the town and state. I would have very few friends in Michigan.

Life for a farm boy, in a defense plant town during a war was quite an experience. There was rationing for things like meat, sugar, butter, shoes, fuel, and tires. Because the plants worked around the clock, movie houses, restaurants and bars were open 24 hours a day. People moved to these busy cities by the thousands and they would never again be the same. The war had many high costs.

A beautiful summer slipped away. The leaves were now falling and the days getting shorter. The farmers market at the edge of town displayed a bountiful variety of products from the locals. I was impressed with the way farmers enjoyed their Saturdays at market. I was getting used to Michigan and I liked it.

My induction notice arrived from the Department of War in October 1943. It was my first letter from the President I never liked. In about a week I would be one of many who climbed aboard buses that caravanned to Detroit. We arrived after dark. We entered the city on a highway that was lined with used car dealers for miles. We were dropped at different downtown hotels and served dinner. The next morning after breakfast the buses picked us up again and we were transported to a huge commercial building that was divided by temporary plywood walls. There had to be a thousand men in long lines. The scene was somber and orderly and there was a serious feeling to the place. It was as if we were obedient animals being herded from one pen to another. Everyone carried their own folder as we walked around in underwear. At each pen someone would check something and put a stamp on our folder. And once again I would find myself in another small room across the desk from a doctor.

He was friendly and soft spoken, not like the cattle rustlers pushing us through the lines. He too would ask about my childhood health. I had little to contribute because I didn't know. But in the end he too told me there was a heart problem and suggested I see a doctor. He said that he will return my draft folder to Muskegan with a recall in one year. He stated that young men often grow out of this problem.

It is hard to remember what I felt at that moment. The very idea of being drafted was deadly serious to contemplate. But at this young age of 18 to be told that I am physically unfit to be a foot soldier was a shock. I can remember riding back in the silence with my mind blank. On the way to Detroit the buses were noisy with laughter and loud talk. But now it was different, they were now all soldiers with an uncertain future and a war had just caught up to them. When I reached Muskegon my sister and Ed picked me up. I told them there would be a delay in my recall and little else. I couldn't handle a second opinion.

When I returned to the plant for work I had to take copies of my medical draft deferment papers. During WWII there was no mischievous manipulation of the military draft system. There would be few jobs men could hide behind — and absolutely no draft deferments for single men. I was in the system with a due date 12 months down the road.

It would be much later when I would fully understand the foolish decision I made by coming to Michigan to be caught in this geographic area of the country from which to be drafted. The selective service system was broken into areas for better distribution of military manpower. Michigan fell under a group of states where nearly all the men would become infantry and sent to the European theater. After being drafted they would be sent home for one month, then sent to a serious training camp and then deployed overseas. The men from this state would soon find themselves stationed in England to prepare for the invasion of Western Europe on June 6, 1944. Those from this state would not only find themselves in the pending invasion but would also be trapped in the horrors of the Battle of the Bulge in Belgium on Christmas of 1944. In the final count, more men from Michigan lost their lives in this war zone, on per capita basis, than any other state. Why was I spared?

When I went back to work I would be in a new division of the plant, final assembly. In this department I would recognize all these pieces and knew most of them by name and even part number. I also knew the function and where they fit in the engine. This would be to my advantage. My new foreman was Mr. Vern Ruckles, a middle-aged man with a gentle nature and very professional.

Vern would be one more role model who crossed my path. My new job carried serious responsibility, and this farm boy soon earned Mr. Ruckles favor.

One day he came by to invite me to have dinner with his family. When I arrived I was not surprised to see his family was a mirror image of this man. After exchanging friendly family talk, I learned that he had a serious heart condition that kept him out of the service. I thought to myself what a coincidence, but I still never mentioned my problem. I thought this was an opportune time to press my curiosity as to what happened in the engine test cells. What I wanted was to work in that department which was staffed with serious faced older men who received better pay. He answered all my questions but he never gave me the indication that he felt I was hinting for that job. I had been spoiled with his quick offers of transfers but this time I felt a little embarrassed for my presumptuous attitude.

One day at work Mr. Ruckles arrived with a paper in his hand, my transfer to the test cells. I was so unbelievably happy that all my other anxieties seemed unimportant. There was a much more serious attitude with the test cell workers. There was not the chatting and visiting that was common in the assembly department. Maybe they were all deaf from the high noise level.... I was received well, given a long dissertation of what not to do and what to watch out for. It was a dangerous place.

I was only 18 and all the other men in the department were at least 40 and had worked in automotive plants. I had to become old fast. I was always impressed with the stringent demands of the military on the quality of work they required from the defense plants. The men in the service got the best available. Everything the military ordered was tested and inspected.

During the initial test of an engine, trouble must be found immediately before serious damage would occur. I had good teachers but I believe it was my farm-boy background that permitted me to handle this job as though I had twenty years experience.

June 6, 1944 came and it was my 19th birthday, and also the day of the invasion of Europe. I wasn't there! The reports that came back were of terrible losses in deaths of soldiers falling on the open beaches. A well-fortified beachhead had Germans well placed for a shameful slaughter. I was content with my challenging job in the test cells with the old guys. I had escaped the slaughter by a German people gone mad.

It was about October of 1944 when I had my first flying lesson. It was not a serious endeavor but rather a distraction from the seven day work routine. The Muskegon airport had several schools and flying instruction was a civil program that was sanctioned by the war department. The first person I met at the small flying school office was Mr. Travis. In those days small aircraft were quite primitive and most pilots dressed like mechanics in work clothes. But Mr. Travis, dressed like a well-polished salesman. Our first meeting was all business. Immediately I was given all the details of what I would learn and the cost. He gave a couple of small books about basic flight safety and airport rules that I had to learn before my next lesson. At that time it took eight hours instruction to solo and thirty five hours of solo time for a private license, — it was a simpler world back then. Most small airplanes had no radio and were bare bones basic.

We took a walk around the small airplane. It was a shiny side-by-side two place Taylor Craft. He thoroughly described what everything did and made ready for our first lesson. My first lesson was my first ride in an airplane. After we were well clear of the ground he told me to fly. I remember thinking learning to fly was no big deal. And after my first lesson I thought it was a little disappointing.

Mr. Travis was an excellent teacher. For him teaching was serious business. Every time he talked you could learn something. The tone of his voice was, "I'm going to tell you once." After my first lesson he asked some specific questions about my work schedule and availability. He suggested I come every other day for a half-hour lesson. He said I would learn to fly much faster and be more coordinated. I agreed. He reminded me to read the small books and said, "I'll see you day after tomorrow."

The half-hour sessions slipped by all too quickly. What I remember most was his strong emphasis on the dangers of stalling an airplane that could result in a spin or a dangerous landing. And that we practiced often. A spin was a strange sensation. It felt like traveling down a fast elevator in a spiral. His big emphasis was to be sure you stayed away from other aircraft. There was no time for idle chatter with Mr. Travis. His most severe critique of my flying was to keep the wings level with the earth.

One day I arrived for my eighth lesson. Each lesson was only one half-hour long. This lesson would complete my fourth hour of instruction. Mr. Travis asked for my log book and after a quick review he made some entries and handed it back. We taxied down to the end of the Muskegon airport runway and received the green light for takeoff. I was told to take off, leave the airport area and reenter the traffic pattern for a full stop landing. After landing he told me I was to taxi back to the end of the runway. As we approached the turn around spot I was told to pull clear of the runway and stop. Then he asked for my log book again. He made several quick entries and returned it. As Mr. Travis opened the cabin door he said, "O.K. Bill, take off and fly around for a half hour." In near shock I questioned the arithmetic, but all he said was, "You're ready, go I'm saving you some money." In less than four hours I had soloed.

It would be months later when I would meet another flight instructor in the airport coffee shop. After some friendly airplane and weather talk he finally said, "Are you Bill?" I answered that I was and he proceeded to tell me he lost a $20 bet to Mr. Travis. The bet was that he could teach someone to safely solo in four hours. We had a conversation about Mr. Travis' teaching ability and decided there was no risk. He did remind me never to mention the incident. I never did.

I do not mention these two incidents of my time in the test cells or my flying lessons to point up any special gift of intellect, I was only an average North Dakota farm boy. I, like all farm kids, grew up with responsibility and discipline. Unlike children today, my day was not spent amusing myself with endless play. We were taught that we contributed to the needs of our family.

The men of that time were not war protestors. They served with patriotism and bravery. At that time there was no room for the simple-minded of the 'Hippie Generation'.

I carried my childhood training of responsibility to California a decade later. It was here that people respected my initiative and energy and I was rewarded well, because of my roots of discipline.

It was March of 1945, I had not heard from the draft board. The war raged on in both Japan and Europe. The constant roar of the test cells was becoming stressful and I was getting homesick and lonely. For 20 months I worked seven days a week. I gave notice to my department head that I was going to quit. In the process of clearing I was sent to personnel where they brought out my personal file as well as my draft status records. The person waiting on me told me I have a draft deferred job. She also added that if I quit I would lose it. I never knew I had a deferment. But it would be canceled immediately and I would be back in the hands of the draft board.

For over a year Mr. Ruckles was a man I would see very often like he was responsible for me. Hardly a day went by that he didn't stop by to ask how I was. He was one of my very few friends and a wonderful role model. When I went to say good bye to him I did not mention my deferment. I knew it could only have come from him and most likely he saved my life. The men from Michigan paid a high price for the war in Europe.

I left Muskegan by bus with only my clothes and a few tools, many I have to this day, I was excited to leave. I can remember nothing about that trip. I can't even remember going back through Gary, Indiana and Chicago. I can only remember that Minneapolis was cold when I arrived. I found the same hotel I stayed in on my first trip and I also found the same cafeteria, the Forum. My transportation was the streetcar and I had no intention of looking for a car with the draft board still owning my future.

I got a job in Minneapolis with Mid-Continent Airlines. The engines on their aircraft were similar to the ones I had worked on in Michigan so I had an open door. I went to work immediately with a real daytime job of only six days a week. I had to stay in the hotel for awhile until I found a place to live. It was real living, my own bathroom, laundry service (there were no Laundromats then) and wake up calls. In about a week I answered an ad for a board and room, very common during that time, that turned out to be the best in town. It was located on 35th and Park Ave., an area that today is a thriving slum in Minneapolis. It was a beautiful large home from another era. I would be only one block from the street car that I would catch to the airport. My new residence would bring another important person into my life, Mrs. Opsal. Her parental qualities and friendship added to my quality of life in many ways. I am only sorry I never told her so.

My new boss at the airlines was Mr. Ted Demick. He would be one of these people you grew to like more every day. I had learned my job well at the war plant and it wasn't long I had the best job he could give me. My department leader was Mr. Les Barkla. He was a very capable person who made my life and work easy. He knew why I was without a car and he and his wife were always taking me somewhere. My new job also would lead me to meet many great people I would one day need, one was, Mrs. Lou Fagerstrom. If I ever missed any attention from my mother, she certainly made up for it. She was a clothing designer and the war department had taken over the plant in which she worked. She chose to work for Mid-Continent, cleaning and testing aircraft engine spark plugs. One of my fellow workers was Bert Larson. He was never drafted because of a serious heart condition. I would be invited many times to his parent's home for Sunday dinner.

Bert Larson and his parents made a big impression on me. They were people of great faith who caused me to realize that this was something I never received from the prairie people of North Dakota....

Overnight I had a family. In August 1945, the war ended. In May, Germany was forced to quit and in August, Japan followed. There was a great celebration in Minneapolis that shut the city down for a whole day. It was a war not soon forgotten.

In September 1945, I received a letter from the new president, Mr. Truman. It requested my presence in the occupation force. This time I was accepted. The desirable U.S. Air force was still blocked to enlistment but because of my aviation experience I was assigned to that service. For twenty months I would belong to another authority and marking time.

CHAPTER FOUR
Into Each Life

From the time I left the farm I had been waiting for the heavy hand of the military to lay claim to my life. When it finally happened it was a relief. It meant I would serve my time and be free. No more checking the mail box for bad news and no more living from day to day. I resigned myself to the idea it would be an adventure.

For me, at the time, the military was a waste of my time. But another day I would find them there to manage a crisis in my life in a way no one else could. There is no equal to the American military, either in equipment or personnel. However, I was never cut out to be a soldier. I am fiercely independent and I am not a team player. These attributes would never serve the military well but it does make for an interesting life.

The process of induction into the military has always been a time of confusion. The haphazard process would lose me for almost a month. Everyone I came in with had long ago been shipped out. When I convinced them that they must have lost my records they agreed. They did and yes, I was lost. The only consolation was that my inoculation record was in my wallet. (At that time the military recycled needles.)

Again someone must have been looking after me. I would have to take all the tests again that would determine placement. Of course it helps to take the Military I.Q. test the second time and another shot at it gave me a high number. I felt like a real loner going through this entire process but it worked out to my favor. I was called into a captain's office as he reviewed my new records. He determined that with my background in aviation that there would be no need to place me in tech school and I would only have a short six weeks of basic training in Texas and then sent to an air base.

I arrived at Kelly Air Force Base practically alone. Usually military recruits come from an area as a group. I would instead be assigned with a group of rowdy and undisciplined young men from New York. They were a group of young Italians that looked for one thing, fun and trouble. The military had little tolerance for the foolish antics of immature boys. Neither did they bother to ferret out the guilty but rather punished the entire unit. Punishment was usually cleaning latrines and kitchen duty. I spent considerable time in these two places suffering the punishments of others. It was a good lesson that taught me to choose my company carefully.

During my short time at Kelly Field I would meet a young man from New York. He was in the bunk next to me. He was well mannered and very quiet compared to the gang he arrived with. He had a heavy clump of dark black hair and was Jewish. His name was Marc. Life for him turned bad when one Saturday morning he went to temple. When the Italians knew he was Jewish they piled on him as though he was a leper. It was my first experience with such bigotry. I became Marc's friend and I know if I met him today I would still recognize him.

After I left basic training, I rode on a troop train for the last time. When I reached California I was assigned to the Army Air Transport service and sent to Hawaii. In 1946 transport planes were slow and inefficient but that was all they had. Because of my experience in aircraft I had the pleasure to travel from California into the far Pacific and back on a C-54 transport for the next 18 months.

I would travel from California to Hawaii where I spent about seven months. At that time Honolulu was a magical place that lived up to the stories by Jack London and Robert Louis Stevenson. The fabled old 'Trade Winds' bar in downtown Honolulu still remained as described by the old storytellers. The bar was an airy, open structure with its interior lined with bamboo and brass lanterns. By chance I would meet my old high school friend, Boyd Hjalmarson.

By that time the military was put on a 40 hour work week, so I had plenty of time to explore the island. I purchased an ancient prewar Salisbury scooter which gave me mobility. The beach of Waikiki had only about four hotels. The grand Royal Hawaiian Hotel had been used by the military during the war but now was given back to the tourists. The beaches were a beautiful sight amidst wide open spaces that have since been filled in. I became totally immersed in the beauty and the balmy weather, and told myself I would return....

I was part of a flight crew on an old C-47 that carried mail and freight. It was a step above an old coastal freight boat but it gave us plenty of low-elevation trips over these beautiful islands. Often we had

Bill as a flight mechanic, U.S.A.F.

The author at Hickam Field, Oahu in 1946.

Bill Vivatson at Clark Field Airbase, Philippines, 1947.

a layover in Hilo and the crew spent a night at the old Naniloa Hotel. It was an old wooden structure set among huge Banyan trees and lagoons. The island was a beautiful place locked in a time of the old cane and pineapple plantations.

Volunteers were sought to transfer to Haneda Air Base in Tokyo. I grabbed the opportunity and sold my faithful scooter and left for Japan. For decades we have had the ease of Pacific travel by taking a 747, nonstop anywhere in the Pacific. In 1946 the old C-54 would be carrying mail and military personnel to places like Johnston Island, Wake Island, Guam, Saipan and Iwo Jima. It was a long slow trip. We spent about three nights on layover. The devastation of war was still evident and large junk yards scattered the shoreline. This was a silent reminder of the price that was paid for these islands. I would be based for a few months at Haneda Air Base located on the ocean shoreline between Tokyo and Yokahama, a distance of about 40 miles. Downtown Tokyo had been spared from total devastation and many old buildings still remained. However as I headed south from Tokyo the entire city was bombed flat to and including Yokohama. The only structures that remained standing were smoke stacks.

I remember how poor everyone was and how little they had to eat. It was hard to believe that these primitive people could be our enemies and how deadly successful they had been. Their dress, life style and actions had the appearance of a terrified people. I had the opportunity to travel by train to some of the coastal cities and everything and everyone reflected a state of misery. I have never had a single moment that I would even consider returning to Japan. My days dragged in this place until I had a chance to transfer to Clark Air Force Base in the Philippines. Today this place lays silent under volcanic ash in the shadows of Mount Pinatubo.

The Philippines was a place where the worst atrocities of the Japanese Government would happen. No matter whether soldier, man, woman or child, all suffered for years. The Filipino people had been shoved into civilization by the wars of the Spanish and American militaries.

These were a primitive and poor people in a war-torn land where time now stood still. I tried hard to travel in my spare time but it was a dangerous and threatening place that I soon wanted to leave but couldn't. There would be no transfer left for me.

One hot miserable day orders came that my unit was being declared surplus. Like a whirlwind, I was on my way to California and home. If there was one single thing that my time in the military proved was that, except for Hawaii, the Asia/Pacific nations were an uncivilized place of misery, corruption and danger.

I was flown to an air base in California. In a single day I was a civilian. I was given airline vouchers to return to North Dakota and was soon on my way home. But in the typical foolish haste of youth or the clever manipulation of the military I foolishly signed documents that would enlist me in the Air Force Reserves.

When I arrived at the farm it was spring in full bloom. It is a time when North Dakota is at its best, just before the mosquitoes arrived to eat you alive and before the time the snow will fall again. After a few days, I told my family I was going to try construction in Minneapolis for now. My time in the service entitled me to a generous plan for college education. It would include tuition, books, housing and other assistance. For so many years, my life had been in the control of others so that for once I wanted some freedom.

My father generously gave me a new truck with the comment that I never asked for anything and that my siblings had received favor. I had been saving my money and bought all new tools and I had a little cushion left over. When I reached Minneapolis, I moved back in Mrs. Opsal's rooming house. I promptly printed up some business cards and headed out to the new tracts to advertise.

The war was over and people were spending money on new projects. It was this long pent-up demand for builders that would give me a start. I had never worked for a contractor and it is now hard for me to believe the unabashed confidence I had at that time. Even my uncle Fred, who lived in Minneapolis, confided to my father that I would be broke in a few months. I was young, naïve, confident and tough. If I would have been smart I would have prayed, "Lord, help me!"

Somehow with fools luck or intervention by chance I would soon be working full time. Fortunately the jobs were small and things I could handle by myself.

I eventually found a niche market that established my new career. This niche market was called the TV room or den. Minneapolis people are very much into their parlors or living rooms. It was a place to show off their 100 percent wool broadloom carpeting, double-lined drapes and expensive furniture from Daytons. It could not be used for such a fad as a TV set.

It was a seldom used bedroom or even the conversion of part of the basement that would become the new den. This room took on its own character that included real hardwood paneling and built in bookcases and a wet bar. Special soundproofing for ceilings and heavy carpeting would be used. Recessed light had become the thing and the den was in demand.

Later I worked at a project where the owner furnished his electrician. His name was Jerry Besner. He was impressed enough with my handling of hardwood that he suggested I call his brother who was building a new house and wanted his den paneled. Mr. Besner owned one of the largest flower import businesses in Minneapolis. After a short meeting I had the job. The Besner brothers were not just anybody, they were professionals and happened to be Jewish. This was a time that anti-Semitic attitudes ran high in America but for me they were a people like anyone else. Past lessons had made an imprint in my life of lasting value.

Prior to WWII, North Minneapolis was the Polish and Jewish ghetto. Minneapolis was well entrenched with the Scandinavian community that still tended to recognize the importance of roots rather than ability or the belonging to the right family. A new development in west Minneapolis called St. Louis Park became an upscale community where the Jewish achievers were welcome. It was through my new friend Jerry Besner that a door would open for me to serve these people. It also was a foretelling of how my relationship with these people would set a course for my life and career. For now it was one day at a time.

A nail-by-nail story of my work is unimportant. What is important are the special people who gave me a chance. All were Jewish. Two that I remembered were Randolph Light, the owner of the largest Studebaker dealer in Minneapolis, and Mr. Capp, who was the largest producer of factory prefabricated homes in the surrounding states. There was another couple, Dr. and Mrs. Goldstein, who chose me to remodel a portion of their colonial home for a study. It had a traditional look of deep-set, small-paned windows and picture-framed paneling. It was a project that pushed my ability. The Goldsteins were my promoters and my friends.

Taking into account the negatives of being self-taught and only a young 24 years old, my success was amazing. I would love my work six days a week and my peers envied me. Little did they understand my anxieties about working at projects over my head or when I would get my next job. Perhaps I made it look too easy and maybe I was too young to be fearful.

About midsummer of 1949, I was traveling by the beautiful Lake Calhoun Parkway out to St. Louis Park. For some time I foolishly envied my friends who had either completed college or were attending. Had I reached a place that I would let others influence my thinking? Or had I lost sight of the value of my inherent gift of ideas and the power of a pair of hands that could build things. In the end it would not matter. There would be circumstances beyond my control where I would forfeit the blessing of being able to manage my destiny.

By August I decided to go to college and use my G.I. Bill benefits. I would attend the University of Minnesota School of Architecture. The pre-entry exams were the last week of August. I was excited about my decision and started the tests. Things went well except for tests with time limitations. One day I felt my sight was very inadequate and when I went home I looked into the mirror for trouble. I could see nothing wrong. I went and told Mrs. Opsal of my plight. She gave me a quick reading test in each eye and found I could not read with one eye. She promptly called her opthalmologist and I had an appointment for the following morning.

As I sat in the doctor's office waiting my turn I simply imagined myself wearing glasses and adjusting to the nuisance. It was soon my turn and after some initial questions by the doctor he looked into my eyes with his examination light. It was only a short moment and he asked me, "Are you a veteran?" I responded yes. He said he would be right back but it took awhile and when he returned I was not ready for his reply. And that was, "You are to report to Fort Snelling veteran's hospital, and take a bag because I don't think you will be released very soon. You appear to have serious trouble."

There are and will be times in all of our lives when everything just comes to a stop. I was not prepared to even ask questions. I couldn't even imagine what could be wrong. I don't remember what I felt or said. My freedom lasted only 16 months. When I went home I felt the dread in the silence of Mrs. Opsal. She must have called the doctor. Our usual lively dinner time was guarded silence.

The next morning someone drove me to Fort Snelling Hospital. I don't remember who. The days that followed were typically that of military paper shuffling. It was several days until I saw a doctor. When I did it was Dr. Brandt and he would be my assigned doctor. I went through the process of a physical and I would have to undergo a spinal tap. It is a miserable procedure with a needle the size of a coke bottle. The negative side effects would be severe headaches that required me to lie flat on my back for hours.

A few days later, Dr. Brandt came to my bed and told me, "We believe you have Multiple Sclerosis. The only treatment we have is histamine solution I.V.'s and we hope it will arrest the progress of the disease." Within minutes a nurse arrived with a stand and an upside down bottle containing a yellow substance. The instant it dripped into my arm there was a strange taste in my mouth. This would happen five days a week for a whole month.

The treatment did not work. The old hospital was of WWI vintage. Tall ceilings and very tall windows surrounded the ward. Placed high on the wall between the windows were large black oscillating fans with black cages. Within the month I saw the fans all slowly disappear. Soon I would lose all usable sight and my life would drift into a foggy haze where I could not read anything or recognize anyone. Once again the responsibility for my life would slip into the hands of another.

My friends were all frequent visitors. The Fagerstroms tried so hard to find things I could use, like a large magnifying glass I still have. Jerry Besner came to see me one day with a stack of magazines. I was not alone. Dr. and Mrs. Goldstein were frequent visitors and they always knew what I needed.

As I reflect back I know I handled the crisis very well. I don't remember crying or lying in bed at night in despair of the future. Maybe it was because I was a 'kid of the prairie'. Life taught us that there was enough trouble for everyone. No one would escape, so learn to adjust.

When my parents arrived I was glad to see them. But I soon came to understand that they carried a greater burden than I for my future. Our meeting was difficult. Both my sisters were R.N.'s and had coached them on my prognosis.

As the days slipped by and the coolness of fall set in, I could almost imagine the ground covered with leaves. The days got shorter and nothing changed for me. I was sure that I would do just as well at home at Opsal's. There was nothing I could do but wait. One day the Fagerstroms brought me a small battery portable radio. It became my constant companion. I was blessed with so much company that one day the head nurse came and told me she was restricting my guests.

There were to be two more spinal taps and I said, "No more." I had a feeling they were practicing. By now the disease had taken my useful sight and also the reflexes of my right arm and leg were deteriorating. I would start walking around the wards to exercise as I didn't want to lose my mobility. I wandered around the hallways with the radio in my ear and looked for someone to talk to....

The days slipped by into late November. One day Dr. Brandt came to my bed with a letter and placed it in my hand. He said the staff agreed that it appears the disease is in remission and that it is best that I go to a warmer climate. He said the letter is to admit you to the Veterans Hospital in Van Nuys, California. He said my discharge papers will be ready shortly and I should leave for California as soon as possible. I had accepted things as they were and there would be no second opinion. Later I asked someone to read Dr. Brandt's letter. It was to introduce me for admission to the hospital. My diagnosis, acute Multiple Sclerosis.

The Fagerstoms had a big going away party for me at their home. The feeling of being away from the hospital made me feel very uncomfortable. The voices were confusing and there was too little detail left in my sight to feel comfortable with my surroundings. In a couple days the Fagerstroms drove me to the farm in my blue van truck. They spent the night on the farm and headed back on the train the next day. My father promptly made a space for my truck in one of the equipment sheds and there it sat until the following summer.

The author's father, "Bobo" Vivatson

It was very uncomfortable to be out on the farm with my family. No one would ask how I felt or what I would like. No one discussed my future or made any suggestions. I felt so alone. There was little question about the stories of the settlers. They were a living testimony that there was pride in strength. The pain of suffering was not a community affair.

This was the time that I felt the weakness of the people I grew up with. I could not describe it at the time, but I fully understand today that it was their lack of simple faith. The entire county was made up of Lutherans and Catholics. They were a people totally void of any Biblical knowledge that was aggravated by superstition and tradition. In that time an important wedding gift was a huge and ornate family Bible. In the front were many lined pages for family records. It was also the filing cabinet for all the import papers like birth certificates and land deeds.

There was never any discussion of the person of 'God' around the household and soon even small children learned to not discuss this topic. The bravado of men was best recognized with their ability to curse fluently. The church was an edifice reserved for confirmation of children and funerals. So for me right now, this painful journey in my life would be a solo trip.

In the few days before I left there would be great gestures of kindness from my father who expressed his love for me in a way his words never could.... First he would ask me how I would travel to California. My choice was the Greyhound bus. But in a few days an airline ticket would arrive in the mail. Another day he bought me an expensive Remington portable typewriter. Something that I would use for many years. And soon I would be on my way.

My Uncle Bill and Aunt Lorraine would meet me in Los Angeles. I spent a couple days with them and later they drove me to Birmingham Hospital. It was a huge facility that looked like dozens of military barracks joined together with large connecting hallways with ramps.

It was the neurological center for the southwestern area of the country. It was the center where all paraplegics would be sent to learn how to cope with half-functioning bodies and life in a wheelchair. It was also the center that cared for M.S. patients. However I did not meet a single one in the four months I was there. The routine of my new confinement was again a long process that could have been accomplished in one hour anywhere else. I found that most veteran hospitals were human parking lots for problems for which they had no answers.

As I was taken to my ward I was very amazed to see all those wheelchairs propelled by young men up and down the wide corridors. The great numbers were sobering. I was taken to a ward where there were about fifteen beds all filled with bedridden patients. All were still recovering from paralyzing injuries caused by war and many others learning to live with their disabilities. What I saw would be the best therapy for me. I had to know I still had it better than the rest of them. When I arrived they had just finished filming on site the movie, "The Men" starring Marlon Brando. It was a story about a paraplegic.

The management of sight loss is so awkward it is hard to explain. Perhaps the best description is isolation. The first gate of communication is eye contact. It is the first display of friendliness or acceptance. The empty gaze of the sightless will seldom draw conversation from anyone. My experience at the time was loneliness.

At first my meals were delivered to the ward with the other patients. I soon asked if I could eat in the mess hall. It was a place where I made acquaintances because I shared a table with others. I had to sit in the same seat each day. My plate would be placed in front of me with the meat at 6:00, the potato or starch at 10:00 and the vegetable at 2:00. I had my own salt and pepper shaker right in front of me and I would first shake the contents into the palms of my hands to monitor the quantity. Mealtime became a time of socializing for me. Whatever the handicaps of the others at the table were, they soon became my willing helpers, seeing that I was taken care of.

I started wandering the huge maze of corridors each day to distance myself from the odor of a dozen bed-ridden men. The corridors were dangerous places with the hundred or so wheelchair patients. All were young and pushed the wheels fast and recklessly to prove they were normal. I walked around with the small radio at my ear and it became their high sign to watch out for me. The corridors were interesting places for me to spend time. Large and complete barbershops. There was a large PX store that carried everything one could think of. My needs were few. There was a coffee shop where people could visit patients and the list of available services made this place like a small town.

One day I stumbled onto a huge ward with every kind of physical therapy device one could imagine, including a dozen or so huge water therapy tubs. Next to it was a gym where I could hear the banging of punching balls. I followed the noise into the gym and a friendly younger man approached me to help. After a short visit and discussion about my handicap, he said that being hospitalized is very detrimental to physical health. He suggested I get involved with a program of body building. He said he would contact my doctor for permission and to discuss my needs.

Meeting this young man, I am sorry I cannot remember his name, was an immeasurable blessing in my life. My time in the gym was at least an hour a day and five days a week. My instructor was always right by my side; I think he thought I might fall. Every exercise was full effort, total 'reps' and everything had to be done right. By the end of my stay I would jump two clothes sizes and for the first time in months felt I was connected to my body. I felt great and also found the reflexes in my right limbs had improved greatly. About 37 years later I would remember this young man who encouraged the exercise program that had such far reaching results.

The occasion was this. In about 1987, my wife and I operated a bed-and-breakfast in Kona, Hawaii. Our booking agent in Honolulu called to ask if we had a room for one week starting that day. Our new guest was to be a doctor from Germany. The next morning after his arrival I joined him for coffee out on the patio. He said he had just come from Japan and was returning to Germany. The reason for his visit to Japan was that he was lecturing on M.S., his specialty. He said the incident of M.S. in Japan was very high, as it is in Western Europe.

I told him of my experience and quickly he went to his room to return with an examination light. Our professional guest peered deeply into both eyes and quietly responded, "You are a very fortunate man, only one in a 1000 successfully survives M.S." He asked the details of my affliction and the treatment I had received. He said the I.V.'s were useless. But it was my description of my exercise program that was of interest to him. He remarked that so far it was the only therapy that showed any appreciable results. He suggested that the energy of strong exercise caused nerve cells to regenerate.

The author's father on the farm in North Dakota

Summer 1950, the author, funcionally blind, washing his blue van truck he would never drive again

Coincidence or not I will never know. However from my present perspective in life there have been far too many instances where the right people were there for me. I can only believe the young man at the gym was one of them.

The wheels turn slowly but surely at the veterans hospitals. Perhaps there is wisdom in letting time do the healing and for me it would come in late April. I met with my staff doctor and he advised me that I was in full remission and more important that my limb reflexes were improving. The I.V.'s had stopped long ago and he said I would be discharged. I was told the eyes are slow to recover from the damage but they will improve but never be the same. They were right. A bare bones pension had been put in place for me. Slow as these doctors are, they do cover all the bases. He asked about my family situation and suggested I go where someone could help me. Soon I was gone.

My stay in California was memorable and one day it would beckon me back. California had already become a magnet for many people from the colder climates. Both friends and relatives had made the move and were now inviting me to join them for dinners and weekends. One of my high school buddies, Boyd Hjalmarson, would twice pick me up and I spent a weekend with him driving me around. Uncle Bill and Aunt Lorraine visited me at least once a week and at times take me home with them for weekends. Often I visited Aunt Betine and Uncle David for dinner on Sundays. There was an Aunt Sally Anderson whom I had not seen for years. One day she came to see me and said she had made an appointment with a fine eye specialist and if she could take me. Aunt Sally was concerned that I never had a second opinion. A thorough examination by the specialist confirmed my problem was M.S.

It was spring when I returned to the farm. May is a time in North Dakota when you never know what the weather will bring next. It can even snow in June and it did that year. I had a need to do something. My father said the old chicken coop was inadequate and suggested I could build a new one if I wanted. My father and I went for a load of lumber and I would have a good project. I could use all my tools except one; I couldn't read the measuring tape. I built the coop without one. It was a ten-by-twenty foot structure and I am sure it still stands.

My restless nature was becoming a problem. It was better if I could stick around the farm because there is always something happening. There were things that made me very uncomfortable and that would be going to Cavalier. I had not learned to handle my handicap and preferred to be by myself. I would expend great effort to be as normal as possible, even in neglect of safety. Even in Birmingham hospital I refused to carry my white cane to spare me from the crazy wheelchair drivers. My stubborn determination worked and I soon was identified as the blind guy with a radio in his ear.

My radio was great comfort but there was one popular song of the time that embraced a painful message. The song was "When I Fall In Love," by Jerry Southern. It was the second verse, "It will be forever," that brought me grief about my uncertain future. But many years later it became one of my favorites and a song of hope.

My big danger was crossing streets. It took a long time to handle traffic lights in the daylight hours. I would stay close to someone and cross with them. Night time was better. I learned to concentrate on the top light, the red one. I became more confident. There would be no reading a menu when I went into a café so I would order what I was sure they had like, chicken or roast beef. Much later I got used to the idea that people are always eager to help so I started asking for things more easily. Even to this day I have learned that a pleasant question can bring about great results.

The survivability of the human creature is legendary. Our ability to cope may take awhile but it is more quickly established when we must accept, like the paraplegics, that things may not get better. The veteran's hospital staff made sure I understood the full extent of my handicap of M.S. with no encouragement beyond the facts. But I am sure I never would accept their honest appraisal. It would be years later that I understood I had some fire burning in me that would not let me live without hope.

I knew the farm was not the place for me because too many people were too anxious to do things for me. I needed to be more independent. I asked my father if he could drive me back to Minneapolis with my truck. We made it a pleasant two-day trip and once again my truck was parked in a garage to wait for better days. I had high expectations of something and I was not sure what. I often caught a streetcar into town to walk around through different retail businesses and try to figure out what I could do. There must be something I could do that someone would hire me for. After a couple weeks in Minneapolis I found there was nothing for me.

Bill and his mother, Hilda Vivatson

Depression has a road all its own. Of course it begins with a real problem or crisis. But soon I didn't have enough confidence left to fight the odds. When I could not even recognize a face what did I think I could do? Soon the toll was complete and I avoided even those who were my friends. For me a big day was to take the streetcar into town and walk around. I had no room left to pretend.

In August the Fagerstroms would take their annual summer vacation at their Briggs Lake home. For them it was a time of having their friends up to visit and fish. Back then there would always be fish dinners after a day of fishing. They asked if I wanted to come with them. They were wonderful people to be around and I was happy to go with them. In the course of packing there would be too much for their old Chevrolet sedan so I suggested we take my van truck. It was a good change of scenery but I would find myself dragging around from one lawn chair to another. My discouragement was becoming too heavy a burden and my only weapon was keeping to myself.

After about a week I became more tired and sat in a lawn chair gazing at the lake. I went to bed early one evening and later I woke up to the sound of rushing air and a plastic window above my head. I was in an oxygen tent. My consciousness must have returned slowly because I would be awakened by a masked face staring through the plastic asking me how I was. Time went by in my state of confusion and someone told me that I was in the Polio isolation ward. I was alone with an I.V. bottle near the plastic tent and little else. I had polio?

I had no recall of time or persons around me. It would be later that I was awakened by two fully masked men telling me they must make a spinal tap. And again I was alone.

The next incident was the fast removal of the plastic tent, my bedding and everything else. There were several masked people that slid me on a wheeled bed and I was pushed into another ward. After I was resettled in bed and the I.V. dripping, someone came to my bed and told me I had Pneumonia. Before long the Fagerstroms were there, smiling and asking me how I was. They filled in the hours of my lost memory. After I got to bed I would start coughing and when they tried to wake me up I would not respond. They went over to the next door home of the Brodys' and used their phone to call Mrs. Fagerstroms' doctor. He told them to get me to hospital immediately and my blue van truck was my ambulance.

Recovery was fast and once again the front desk had to limit my visitors. Whatever was the reason for me to contract pneumonia I will never know, but the experience of being in the Polio ward was a shock treatment all of its own. At that time Polio was a scourge of the northern plain states. It was a fast moving virus that would cause instant paralysis and death. The old iron lung was a tool of survival at that time. There were no mild cases of polio.

Mrs. Opsal's rooming house was my home again. It was late August 1950 and I was 25 years old. Since I left high school my life had been a calamity of which I had little control, I still had little control, but I had every reason to be thankful.

The next five months became a purposeful whirlwind of activity. I went downtown to the best stores and bought new clothes, expensive clothes. One was a purchase of a very expensive suit from Dayton's and five years later I wore it to my wedding in Los Angeles. I still had not found a job but I was looking. It was autumn and the new cars were hitting the show rooms and I was very interested in what was new. Like a melodrama of what life could be — a taste of hope.

As the snow was starting to fall I had little intention of heading for warmer weather. It was hard enough for me to get along here where I knew people. My Aunt Emma and Uncle Fred had moved to Minneapolis a year ago and they were like family. They extended generous invitations to their home. They were a great help and encouragement to me.

There were some noticeable changes in my eyes where there were some things and some colors I could see well. The color that was most visible was blue. The color blue stood out like it was electrified. In rebellion, I changed my clothing colors to anything but blue.

It was late November when I was walking around Donaldson's Department Store. I was in the appliance and furniture department. I noticed everything had large price tags. All the salesmen had suits and were standing around. I approached them and asked who the supervisor was. They pointed me in the direction of an elderly, gray-haired man. I explained my problem to him and I was immediately given a job. This fatherly man told me to show people what was on the floor and bring them to him to write the order when they made their choice. For now it was what I needed and I was grateful.

It was shortly before Christmas and my curiosity in new cars became a shopping pastime. One day I dropped into the Lake Street Pontiac and saw what I wanted. It was the first of a model called the Pontiac Catalina. A convertible body with a metal top. The body was ivory and the top was rust color with matching leather seats. I went to a gray-haired salesman to ask about the price and if they would take in a van truck. The price was acceptable and yes they would take a trade-in. I asked a puzzled looking salesman to drive me out to see my blue van truck that was parked in a garage. His offering price was bad but he quickly suggested I advertise it in the newspaper. He suggests the asking price as well. I did and the first person who came to look bought my (ambulance) van truck. The next day the same salesman had to drive my new Pontiac Catalina to my garage and park it. Right about now one would have to question if I was a 'nut case' or obsessed.

My hours at Donaldson's were easy but long. From 9:00 A.M. to 5:30 P.M. and 9:00 P.M. Friday night. I looked forward to Sunday when I backed my new car out on a snowy driveway and wiped it down as though I had just made a trip. And when I finished admiring it I started the engine and drove it back into the garage. One such early Sunday morning when the snow covered the ground but the pavement was black and clear I decided to attempt a drive around the block, very slowly. I was excited with my four block trip. It was the first time I had driven in a year and a half. It was best described as a triumphant move of a young man driven beyond common sense.

By the end of December I would start taking late night rides. I found that the contrasts of the nighttime darkness and the glare of street lights permitted me to see well. It would be the best way for me to see stop lights. It was obvious something good was happening. The snow was on the ground but the streets were clear and black. The strong night contrasts of black and white made me feel safe. It is hard to remember what I really saw with my sick eyes but there was never a crisis that I would remember. I told no one of my midnight sojourns.

I went home to the farm for Christmas and there was a different mood. Everyone knew I was doing better and almost every day my father would drive me into Cavalier for coffee or lunch. I wasn't as fearful as before although I was not recognizing faces or reading print other than headlines. After my return to Minneapolis my after midnight trips were getting more and more daring. If it would have started to snow I would have been in big trouble. I depended on contrast to see well. The word got out among my friends about my late night rides and I received little encouragement for my foolish escapades. I was still working at Donaldsons and the long hours kept me busy with my own concerns. It must have been late January or February when I made my first early Sunday trek into the country west of Minneapolis, an area I knew very well. I learned to recognize street lights by concentrating on the top light, the red. In the 1950s there were no freeways. Traffic was slower and so were the cars.

It is hard to remember what sparked the idea that I would make a trip by myself. I was starting to identify the disdain my friends exhibited over the brazen confidence I was exhibiting. I am sure that I was losing favor with my peers and the bridge widened. I imagine this fired my enthusiasm to make a trip even more. My unbelievable plan would take me out of Minneapolis to Hopkins where I would take the highway southwest across the southwestern end of South Dakota into Nebraska where I would pick up Route 66. I could not read a map and I could not read the instrument panel. I was living my life on the fringe and alienating those who loved me.

My measured recovery was under way with or without my forceful motivation to make things happen faster. For now no one could change my mind and even if professional concern was available, I wouldn't listen.

It was a day in late February I received a call from Aunt Emma. She put my mother on the phone. My parents had just arrived from the farm and she invited me for dinner. It was good to see my parents but I was suspicious about their trip. The conversation soon switched to me. My parents said they were here, bags packed, to drive me and my new Pontiac Catalina to California. My ego-charged plans hardened my concern or sensitivity for my parents. I lied appropriately to assure them I had no plans to take a trip. In a few days, my distraught parents took the bus back to the farm. I was amazed at the callousness and disregard I had for their feelings. It was a foolish plan of escape.

CHAPTER FIVE

Putting the Pieces
Back Together

It was February 1951 that I knew my eyes were beginning to improve. It was my distance vision that made it easier for me to get around.
I still had a job in furniture sales at the Donaldson's Department Store.
I know it was a place that was made for me and I will always remember
their generosity. By now there was a legion of those who loved me and
attempted to keep me cheered and busy on my slow progress back to
health. I am certain they felt my insecurity about my future and made
every effort to include me in their activities. I still felt alone and I
found more comfort in my determination to keep busy than pretend-
ing everything was all right. Determination was becoming my primary
weapon of recovery.

My obsession now would be to take my new car out for a ride late at night. I would remember my location by memorizing building shapes or counting streets or intersecting roads. I could not read the street signs unless I left the car. In the last few weeks before my departure I had ventured out into the country by using the smaller county roads. As I became more emboldened with my high-risk driving habits I knew it was time for me to leave.

I had sold my tools as I had no idea when I could use them again. My sparse belongings were my clothing and typewriter. Mrs. Opsal had been very quiet. There were no petitions of waiting or staying a little longer. I don't even remember if she told me to be careful. It was a simple hug with few words that made our feelings known to each other. She was a special friend. I would never again see her alive.

I drove out to Hopkins and headed west, the direction of California. The snow spotted the countryside and the contrast of black pavement gave me considerable confidence. I recognized road sign shapes such as stop signs. Courage is a strange measurement of human strength. For me it was the simple fact I had few options.

I would get the road numbers at a Hopkins filling station that led through South Dakota, Nebraska and to the famous Route 66. I was told that the best winter route would be to drop south through Denver to the desert country and into southern California. It sounded so easy this first day but much later I often wondered what protective hand was my traveling companion. It proved to be a dangerous trip.

The deficiency in my sight left my close range vision almost useless. I could recognize no one unless they were very close. There was no use to write anything down because it was so blurred I could not make out the writing. Things I learned from my many stops at filling stations would have to be trusted to memory. My distance sight was an issue of watching contrasts and forcing myself to study shapes and objects. I would never pass any vehicle no matter how slowly they traveled, even farm equipment. As I write this I have to ask myself, was I really crazy?

Looking back, this trip began 53 years ago. I don't remember whether my spirit was one of high adventure or not. I can only recall the trials I endured from the trip as I pressed west, very slowly and very alone. It was necessary to establish a routine that assured my safety. It was the filling station men and truck drivers who became my partners in this silent journey.

I learned to recognize filling stations, and refueled very often because the gauges were illegible. The stations would be my source of information. Time to destinations meant little as I was still unable to read a watch. But what I can remember best was stopping hundreds of times to double check road signs. Days would simply drift by because there were no newspapers or anything else to track time. The car radio was my companion. There would be no phone calls or letters. It was a journey measured by endurance and not common sense.

The safest time to drive was late at night when the traffic was low. The contrast of the black pavement and the lights made driving easy.... Truck stops were the best places to fill up with gas and ask if I could park and spend the night. A truck stop usually was where to find a café and road information. The nights were always very cold. I never slept in a bed until I reached Colorado Springs. My comforter was the long overcoat I bought at Dayton Company. The traffic was very heavy. All highways were only narrow two lanes of pavement with no shoulders. The trucks were slow so I would follow them for miles. I would soon find out that truckers were aware of my presence. Very often as I followed them into a filling station the driver would come over and ask if everything was all right. I soon learned to ask them where they were going and if I could follow. I am certain they knew I had some sight problems. My request for help from the truck drivers would never be rejected. It was a strange alliance that to this day I cannot explain.

The only life-threatening incident that I would find myself in was about 75 miles north of Denver. It was early evening and the traffic was very heavy. I chose to pull off the two lane roadway and rest. As I did so, there were at least two sets of railway tracks I would have to cross to reach an open space where I parked. Stopping and resting was sort of a recharging therapy for my eyes and I did it often. This night I waited a long time for the traffic to get lighter.

When I decided to move on there was a very long string of cars and trucks in each direction. The lights appeared as one solid beam of glare. I slowly eased over the tracks looking for a break in the lights. I moved slowly across the last track to look for an opening in the line of traffic. In a split second there was a tremendous blast of a horn that coincided with an earth-shaking rumbling roar directly behind me. The frightening weight and speed of this train was a scare beyond description, but it was not my time.

It was late evening when I reached Denver. The route that I chose took me to desert country was through Colorado Springs. The elevation was very high and very cold. Again it was another filling station man who would give detailed instructions of how to drive to Colorado Springs. The trip was on clear roads but large snow banks lined the roadways. I arrived very late. I pulled off to the side of a safe road and went to sleep. Sometime during the dark early morning a friendly policeman woke me up to see if I was alright. I told him my plans and he said there had been heavy snow in the area and that my route was not safe. I asked if there was a reasonable place to stay and he led me there. It would be the first time I slept in a bed since leaving Minneapolis. I had lost track of the days and it felt like a long time. I remember I was so tired and that the little hotel was like a haven to gather my strength.

When my journey continued, I traveled over a pass that had just experienced considerable snow fall. My ability to handle an all-white world meant trouble for me. As I made my way up the pass there was snow on the roadway and I became confused. I hit a small snow pile that grabbed my right front wheel and pulled me into a snow bank. I was stuck. Within a minute a huge truck pulled up behind me and stopped. He asked if he could help. I told him the bright sunlight on the snow was a problem for me.

Without hesitation he said he would pull ahead of me and pull me out to the clear roadway. He said my route choice was bad until we reached lower elevations. He suggested I follow him down. Some time later he pulled into a road side café and I followed. The truck driver and I had lunch together. He asked many questions and must have wondered what I was doing in this part of the country. Whatever he thought of me, it turned out I would follow him for hours. He was going as far as Boulder City and I could follow him. When we came to a stop at a big intersection a big sign read, Salt Lake City. I asked the truck driver if the road was mountainous and how far to Salt Lake City. He assured me the road was good and little chance of snow. It was good to have his company if for only a day. I said good-bye to my guardian angel and chose to make Utah my stop for awhile.

As I moved in the direction of Salt Lake City, I instinctively knew my odyssey must end for now. It wasn't difficult to reach Salt Lake City, as it seemed there was only one road, no snow, and not cold. I don't remember being disappointed about my change of destination. I am sure I had become used to accepting things as they are and not what I would like.

As I headed north toward Salt Lake City the traffic was light, unlike Route 66. The small towns were very far apart and I had to wonder what people lived on. The entire distance to Salt Lake City looked like barren land. It was an easy trip into the city of wide and orderly streets. I kept my eye out for my good friends at the filling stations and soon I found an attendant with good information and directions. I asked him where there were places to live and if there were any jobs. He suggested I go to Ogden, only about 30 miles north. He added that Hill Air Force Base was hiring and they were overhauling B-29's and A-26's for the Korean War. The Korean War developed so quickly that it would be fought with WWII equipment.

As I headed north to Ogden, I was asking myself what I was doing here. Utah was a place that held no interest for me at all. I suppose I had heard some of the negatives of the Mormon people that had already prejudiced my opinion. I tried to console myself that this was a place to rest up and then go on to California.

Ogden, like Salt Lake City, was easy to enter. Very wide uncluttered streets would take me right into town. At the main crossroads of downtown was a brick hotel, a movie theater and a Chinese restaurant. I parked and went into an old but attractive hotel and rented a very reasonable room for a weekly rate. The Chinese restaurant was very good and not at all like my first introduction to Chinese food in Muskegon. That was, everything on the plate tasted the same.

After a good nights rest and a new day of sunny skies made me feel better. It was the first of March and spring would come early to Ogden. The city sat at the base of the Rocky Mountains that were a very attractive backdrop. A walk around town convinced me this was not a bad place at all.

In Ogden you only had to ask questions for what you wanted. For now I knew I had to save money and I asked about renting a room. Immediately I had a name and address of someone who had a room close by. I rented in a home with two older sisters living with their mother. They were wonderful people. Both the sisters were school teachers and every morning they would set breakfast out for me. I was enjoying my escape from the road. The house was only a couple blocks from main street and I found it best to park the car for awhile and walk.

I would eat dinner almost every night at the Chinese restaurant. They had a big menu that offered basic foods and most of the town ate there.

I decided it was time to look for work at Hill Air Force Base. My weak eyes had taken a setback so I made a very cautious trip by car to the huge facility. By asking many questions, I found the personnel office to apply for a job. I must have had a considerable amount of nerve to think I would get a job working on military aircraft when I couldn't even read the job application form. But before long I found myself in the hands of a couple more guardian angels. When I first spoke to the desk person I explained my handicap and asked if there was some kind of work I could do. Very quickly I was ushered into an office to speak to a friendly gentleman who asked me many questions.

At that time all the doors were open to veterans and this man willingly filled out my application. There was no discussion of what I could do. My former aircraft experience was listed and I knew I could not do this sort of work now. When he finished my application he made a phone call. He said he had to talk to someone and I waited at his desk. I knew I was asking for more than was reasonable and I think I was prepared for "I am sorry." When he came back he asked me to come with him. As we walked out of the austere military style employment offices we came into an area of big offices and nice furniture and very well-dressed people. We reached a desk with a secretary. I was ushered into a very expensive looking office and introduced to the man behind a large desk. A well-dressed man arose to shake my hand and asked me to sit down. He dismissed my escort and we were alone.

I remember very well that I knew I was in the presence of someone very important. I would find out days later I was right. For whatever reason, this person chose to find me a job who must have had more important things to do. In a few minutes I was walking through the entire huge plant with him. Parts of disassembled B-29's were everywhere. After looking at all the job possibilities I chose the department that replaced deicing boots on large sections of B-29 wings. It was something I could handle.

I will always remember this well-dressed fatherly figure walking me around this large facility with his hand at my elbow as though I might fall. There are times in everyone's life when a 'guardian angel' has interceded on their behalf. For me it was a memorable experience, one that is treasured throughout a lifetime. The kindness expressed by this complete stranger is so memorable that it seems it was only yesterday. But by now there were so many such incidents that I have to understand I was walking with angels. I have no other explanation.

As I look back at this incident I cannot help but understand there is an important lesson here. That is, too many people live in a state of constant fear. They are afraid to ask for something important or reasonable. They live in fear of asking questions. Perhaps they lack the curiosity to know things they can learn by asking. Maybe they don't know how to ask a question. I believe I inherited an important lesson from my father, that is, don't be afraid to ask for something if your request is important and reasonable. Great things can happen by asking in a proper way. Too many fail to permit themselves to be approachable.

I adjusted to Ogden very well. I could walk to town. I ate my share of Chinese food and started going to movies. I started driving again and felt more confidence in this quiet place. The Mormons were very serious and orderly people. I found a small cafe that didn't do Chinese food and they weren't Mormons. They were a good source of information about the Mormon people, their politics and faith. I met a very a nice Mormon girl who was fun to be around. But I soon found that our conditional alliance depended on my accompanying her once a week to the evening youth fellowship, a place where young Mormons were taught to be different. It was so devoid of any message or substance I wondered why they bothered going. I later found another girlfriend who was separated from her husband. She was a 'Jack Mormon'. This is a description of a Mormon who chooses to break rules and not follow instructions. She was enjoyable company until one day I spotted her husband for the first time and I thought it best to stick with a real Mormon for now. He weighed about 200 pounds.

In late March my parents came by train to visit me. They stayed in the only hotel, next to the Chinese restaurant. One day we were driving in the back mountains above Ogden. It was a desolate place and I mentioned to my father that this would be a great place for target practice. The next day he bought me an expensive target rifle and case. There was little doubt that my parents carried a very heavy burden for me.

One day there would be another breakthrough on my road to recovery. I discovered I could read the print, with care, of the June 1951

Recovering from M.S. in Utah, 1951

issue of *Readers Digest*. My sight had improved enough that I felt I would like a different job, I put in for a department transfer to the area that prepared the newly overhauled B-29's for flight and I was quickly moved to the department. It was all outdoor work and Ogden has beautiful summers. The higher elevations keep things cool. There were younger men in the department who were into fishing and camping in the mountains behind Ogden. They were 'Jack Mormons' and their sin was drinking beer. On a long holiday weekend, a group of us went to the Snake River Canyon for a camping trip. What a highlight in my life! It was better than North Dakota. The colorful Snake River Canyon was a wilderness I had never experienced before. The mountains soared far above the racing rocky river and the trees were towering giants. It was far from traffic and people and it was a simple time of enjoying life, it was a boost for my recovery.

Summer slipped away. I looked forward to going to work and my savings had grown. The only love affair I had going was with my car. On my days off I would take long rides in the beautiful back country. I am sure my mind harbored the memory of losing this wonderful blessing and I was making up for lost time.

As the days reached into fall I had to realize this was the wrong job for winter. The air base was right in the downhill draft of Logan Canyon. Already the cold winds were preparing us for winter. I was very well treated by the Mormon people in Ogden. It had been a good summer with good experiences. However, one of the curses of youth is restlessness, and only a few bad mistakes can cure this calamity. I was assembling a list of reasons for moving on. I was alone and there was no one to consult with or reason to stay so I soon would be on my way.

In October I quit my job and made plans to head south for the winter. At that time the only reasonable solution to the problems of M.S. was warmer weather.

Once again I packed up my personal things and drove away. But regrettably my thoughtless and immature nature would never think of collecting the names of all those who helped me in Ogden, and I would never be able thank them. I well remembered a young man named Ted who worked with me on the flight line. He fully understood my handicap and if he thought for a moment I needed help with something he was there. Oh, that I could remember the name of that C.E.O. who treated me like a hurting son.

61

I would survive the mistakes and if there were any redeeming lessons they would be realized at a price. Perhaps that is the only way we mortals can learn. But I was about to make a more costly mistake.

CHAPTER SIX

Twenty Months Wasted
But Lessons Learned

I could easily skip this next segment of my life and pretend it never happened. But instead I would rather recount the mistakes that are repeated by all too many of us. I am sure I was simply lonely and homesick, the seeds of a major mistake.

Minnesota, like all the Midwest states, is a classic example of the enigma called 'roots'. All settlers were from the cold climates of the Northern European countries where one burrows in for the long dark winters with hearth and family. This might serve survival well but it is not a place where souls are set free to discover and develop ones gifts and talents. I lived with these closeted people long enough to know that too much time is spent in gossip, protecting family and jobs and locking everyone else out.

When I was in Minneapolis I had been involved in remodeling. It was a closed community for the trades as well as many other areas of business. One's roots meant everything. Old ideas were good enough for everyone and new energy and talent came in second.

I had to learn that we cannot go backward. Life is an adventure that moves only forward. This is a chronic problem for a great number of us. I remembered the good times. Dinner out with the gang, an evening at the road house, tobogganing and ice skating. Minneapolis was a fun city. But what I found was that the lives of my friends had moved forward and only I was trying to tread water.

My new-found freedom would soon permit me to make a bigger mistake at a loss of 20 valuable months of life, all too soon I forgot about my plans to go to California. I permitted myself to be convinced that there was too much traffic in California. I am sure someone had told me how wonderful Florida was and that the South was a great place. Blindly, I quit my job in Ogden and headed east.

I made my way south to El Paso, Texas, the most westerly point of that state. At that time El Paso was one big intersection in the desert. I came from the north, and south would take me to Mexico. If I turned right California was waiting for me. But like a fool I would turn left for Florida. The monotony of flat and boring landscape went on for several days. I have always found trouble with seeing beauty in the desert. Someone who thinks the coconut is the most beautiful tree is hardly one to describe the beauty of the desert.

As I ventured deeper into Texas, it began to look like scenes in the old western movies. Rolling hills and large oak trees dotted the landscape. In that time Texas was a wide open place. The towns were far enough apart that I cautiously filled my gas tank at every one. I can remember driving for a couple hours and never seeing one house.

There was nothing interesting enough to stop and look. My odyssey stumbled over rolling hill upon hill. How lonely this place was!

In Houston I stopped at the new and beautiful Conrad Hilton Hotel. It had been touted as the first real new hotel in America. As I pulled into the hotel grounds I found myself surrounded with uniformed young men wanting to take my car away from me. My only earthly possession! For the first time in my life my car would be parked by a valet.

I made my way to the restaurant, and it was spectacular. High ceilings and windows that let the full power of the sun wash it in brightness. I ordered something like the chefs salad. It arrived on a turkey platter and I first thought it was a mistake. Soon I had a plate and six pieces of silverware and about four glasses I could drink water out of.

I got over my embarrassment that this was all mine and started somewhere on the turkey-sized platter. I decided selfishly, I was meant to live like this.

It was at this time I began to see the essence of man's creative ability. My eyes drifted from one architectural detail to another. Did I blow my budget, or was the meal worth the price, I don't remember? But I know I was frozen in a moment of appreciating the creativity of professionals that I felt comfortable with. I had enjoyed something new and inspiring.

Eventually I moved east to Texarkana. It was a town that had no outskirts and no downtown, a faceless place with dark dripping clouds that would follow me for a week.

I came to an area that no longer looked like Texas. It was endless miles of causeways and wooden bridges that were too narrow to safely meet a truck. It was a swamp.

Later I could see signs that told me how far I was to New Orleans. This area was always poor but after going through a war everything looked in disrepair. The overcast skies and slow rain only made it look uninviting. I would never know if I was in New Orleans or not, I just drove on.

This was a poor area that could have been industrial or simply nothing. I was on a long bridge when I heard a 'thump, thump', a flat. I pulled to the side and quickly opened the trunk to retrieve the tools and spare. Suddenly a man came running toward me waving his hands. I was on a rotating bridge. He forced me to drive to the center of the control tower for the bridge.

In the safety of the pivot point of the bridge I changed my tire. The bridge tender pointed me to a place where I could repair the flat. The place was an old wooden building with a single gas pump and little else. The attendant told me he could help me but not now. He said I could wait inside.

It was the living quarters of a very poor family and contained a few old chairs, a table and plenty of junk, everything from old tires to quart cans of oil. There were a couple of little kids padding about and a very skinny and poorly dressed woman appeared now and then. I felt like an intruder.

As I sat there I looked at poverty in a way that pained me deep in my heart. It was as though my mind was collecting unforgettable pictures of where I never wanted to be.

Later my tire was repaired and I was back on the rainy and dark roads. I knew I was on a journey I would never repeat. My soul demanded something better at a time when I had little strength left to cope with anything more than my own recovery.

When we travel through a strange place we are slow to grasp problems and conditions related to that place. But the shapeless forms of black humanity trudging on the shoulders of the road began to make me understand. They wore unobtrusive dark clothing. They trudged stoop shouldered and always looking down. They moved like the misery of the world belonged to them alone. And everywhere were the signs, 'whites only'.

Adrift in the rain on narrow roads I soon reached Mobile, Alabama. It's interesting that so much music was written about these southern places but when you witness it first hand the romance of the place disappears.

Soon I left the rain and entered the orchard land of northern Florida. It was sunny, flat and green. Fifty years ago Florida was rural with untold miles of wasteland. There were miles upon miles of orchards and roadside signs advertised 'fresh orange juice, fifteen cents a glass.'

I took a straight shot to the Atlantic and turned south in the direction of Miami. There was a long waterway I think was the Banana River that follows the coast for miles. It was a beautiful tropical coast of open space. I was starting to think that this would be the place to spend the winter. From the highway it looked beautiful and civilized.

Miami, like so many American cities, showed the stress of the wartime years. The honky-tonk looking retailers who followed the military still lined the streets. One of the founders of talk radio was Arthur Godfrey. This guy had painted a picture of paradise and called it Miami. It wasn't so. I stopped for gasoline and asked some important question, like where to stay and is there any work here? I received good directions where to stay but he said Miami was on hard times.

I found a small apartment in a place called Hollywood. It was near a huge open farmers market that not only sold produce but had several open air restaurants. It looked friendly with a big variety of good food.

I had been on the move for days through the south. I had traveled through so much rain I would pay little attention to any social miseries. But now I had stopped in a large working class neighborhood and there the bigotry was more pronounced. Not only were toilets for 'white' and 'black' but also water fountains were also segregated. The colored were permitted to buy at the market but they could never sit down to eat.

It's strange, but bigotry is not so bad unless it touches us personally. When I went out to the Miami airport to look for work, I learned that the 'Yankees' rated a close second behind the colored. I would soon find out at the sociable looking market place that these were bigoted people who made my skin crawl. There was no job for me and I wanted to leave.

I took the coastal route up to Jacksonville and arrived about midday. It was an interesting city, but since there was no place to stop I drove through the center of downtown and parked in an area of apartments and houses. I walked back into town to look around. There was a small park with large trees and some signs that indicated this place was once a slave trading market. I immediately ended my tour of town and headed for my car.

I forgot my way and soon I was completely lost or else my car had been stolen. I dared not think of that possibility. I was walking in circles and didn't know what I could do. How could I tell the police I lost my car. I came upon a church with the front door open. I don't know what I thought they could do, but I walked in. A man approached me to ask what I wanted and I told him my problem. He took the time to ask where I had entered the city and could retrace my tracks. He gave me the address of the church and told me to come back if I didn't find it. He said he would help me.

The pastor started asking me many questions about where I was coming from and what my destination was. I am sure he detected some problems that I could not mask very well. He asked if I needed a place to stay or if I needed money. He told me to come back if I didn't find the car. At the end of our meeting he asked if he could pray for me. He did. I thanked him and said good-bye. I walked right to my waiting car.

The next day in late afternoon I arrived in a rainy Atlanta. At that time the old roadways took everyone right into the center of a city. And this is where I ended up. I stopped for gasoline and asked some usual questions. There were plenty places to stay in Atlanta and I soon learned that the Bell Bomber plant was open in Marietta and was hiring. The hope of a job made me anxious to get to Marietta that was only about 35 miles away. America was deeply involved in the Korean War and the old B-29 was being rebuilt in Marietta.

This was a pleasant little town of about ten blocks in each direction. A dreary rain was falling and all the barren tree trunks looked black. I stopped at a small motel and spent the night.

The next morning it was still raining when I drove out to the big plant. It was a facility that built B-29's during WWII. When I approached the airfield the buildings looked so huge I confused them for clouds. Within half an hour I had a job. I spent several hours going through the employment process. When I went back to the motel I told them I would need a room or small apartment. They sent me to see a couple who rented rooms and I had a nice place to say. I could not help but think of that pastor and his praying for me.

My first day of work was one of amazement at the enormous volume of the place. There were rows of these huge bombers in different stages of overhaul. I was assigned to the section that prepared the newly overhauled planes for delivery.

I soon knew that there would be no job in the south that could keep me here. Scattered about the plant were white signs with black letters by the entry of every toilet and drinking fountain that read, — White Only, — Black Only.

One day at work I made a bad slip. The hangers and working areas were kept clean by janitors who were all black. The only other jobs they were given were in the cafeteria. One day there was a big mess to be cleaned up in our work area and I said, "I'll get the black lady to come and clean up for us." In an instant one of my work mates shot back at me, "Man, what are you talking about? There are black women but there are no black ladies." These would never be my people.

My status as an ignorant Yankee was tolerated and my experience on the B-29's was respected but for sure I would never be counted as one of them. But one day something happened in our section that moved me up in their opinion at least to be their work equal.

The incident occurred one rainless day when the first overhauled B-29 would be delivered to a U.S. Air Force crew for the war zone of Korea. The like-new plane had been test flown a couple times before delivery. There was an aura of serious importance as the large number of important people gathered to witness the delivery and departure of the first overhauled B-29 by Lockheed. There were smiles and hand-shakes by everyone and soon a 'squeaky clean' Air Force crew boarded the aircraft.

All was ready to start the four engines. As each number one, two and three reluctantly coughed and barked to life in a cloud of smoke everyone shared in the excitement of a job well done. But as number four engine was being started it would give a few sputters of life and quickly stop. Several more attempts at restarts failed and then all the other engines were shut down. The crew left the bomber and now everyone was wringing their hands and mechanics were bringing large ladder like stands to check the engine.

I finally got up enough nerve to approach my red-neck boss and his favorite mechanics in attendance. I told them that it sounded like the engine driven fuel pump lines had been crossed. With a glare of scorn he reminded me it had been test flown and my advice was not needed. The boss called for a tall ladder and the engine cowling was removed. Several of the favorite mechanics buried their heads in the big engine for a considerable length of time. Then someone shouted, "The fuel lines are reversed." As my red-neck boss called for some tools, he didn't even look my way. A fast start up of number four engine indicated all was well. There were a new round of hand shakes and slaps on backs and the crew was back aboard. Everyone watched as the bomber taxied down the runway and completed the take-off. My red-neck boss never even approached me to comment on my diagnosis.

This incident was typical of so many in my young life. When I was beaten down and my self-worth was at a low ebb, there came a vindication that gave me comfort. It was as though a quiet voice knew I needed encouragement to keep going.

I soon received a good pay raise and time slipped by and soon it was spring in Georgia. The landscape was ablaze with fruit tree blos-soms. The constant drip of wet and cold was replaced with sunlight and I headed north to Minneapolis.

Coming home would be returning to Opsal's rooming house. Old acquaintances wouldn't be the same, but I thought that this was home. It was not to be.

This year of discontent gave me time to take a good look at the negatives of Minnesota. They were the same ones I had seen over a year ago. In the back of my mind was the nagging of the call to California.

I was kept busy with some very good projects; one would be the complete remodeling of a lake home for a Dr. Giere. He was a wonderful man who appreciated my work and also happened to be Jewish. But there would be one other project that gave me the emotional boost I would need in life.

The project would be a complete remodel of a kitchen and dining area in a classic old home in the good part of town. The entire area was stripped to the bare walls and new large windows were installed. New cabinets and decoration in interesting colors made the place look warm even in winter.

A few months after I had moved to California I received a big package from the owners of the new kitchen. When I opened it, I found a full (large) color front page of the Sunday home section of the *Minneapolis Tribune*. There was an accompanying page that detailed the project and a short story about me.

There is a lesson here that I have not fully sorted out. I know it was a vindication for my mistakes. But how fortunate I was that this story was not published until I had arrived in California. It is possible that if I was in Minneapolis at the time of the article, I might have stayed. And I would have lost the unbelievable future that was waiting for me in California.

CHAPTER SEVEN
California
Where I Belonged

This would be the second time I planned a trip to California. My winter in Minnesota was a difficult one. There had been too much snow, the snow stayed too late and it was a very cold winter. I was finding that my frustration with Minneapolis was not imaginary but real. It was still a place where the old ways of identity were still recognized. The city was growing but the growth was well beyond the city limits. The new suburbs represented inconvenience and too much time spent in travel. The rapid growth was at the expense of a once enjoyable and convenient Minneapolis.

My vision was looking west but there is always that nagging doubt I was making a mistake. Already my life had so many pot holes in it that I had to be careful. In June, I would be 28. My frustrations were deep. I felt that every way I measured my options I knew this was no place for me. My family was still a long 300 miles away and I would not be able to visit often. I had to question if I had fallen into the trap of thinking I needed to live near my roots? If so, there would be no future for me.

There is always that one incident, crisis or confirmation and the choice is made for you. The occasion would be one evening when my friend and I would take our girlfriends for dinner at the Shokopie House in an out-of-town village called Hopkins. What I very much liked about Minneapolis was wide choices of social activities. Shokopie House was just one of them. The city abounded with live theater, exhibits and ice skating in the parks in winter. The city boasted more parks and lakes than any other city. It was something that California would grievously lack.

Shokopie House looked like a huge ranch house in a beautiful setting of mature trees on a hilly site. These places were called 'road houses' back then. They were set up as a restaurant and bar during the week but also they had a large dance floor that was surrounded with tables for dining. On weekends they had live music. For the price of an excellent dinner a group could occupy the table for the whole evening. And there were many such places. And tonight I would enjoy this setting with my friends.

As our fun continued later into the evening, we started to notice people coming in with a good dusting of snow on their clothing. It was the first of April, too late in the season for a snow storm. But later there was an announcement that for those without tire chains it was time to head home. Home was 20 miles away and we weren't worried about the snow. Fun comes first.

As we left Shokopie House the road was well covered with snow and it showed little sign of stopping. Fortunately, the Saturday night traffic made enough tracks to make the roads passable. But as we reached the city the snowplow trucks were all busy shoving the heavy snow to the sides of the road. A long circuitous route would get everyone home and that left me alone to drive back to Opsal's. I was several miles from home and found myself firmly locked in deep snow with no chains. Any attempt to ram the car back and forth to make my own path was unsuccessful.

I can only remember leaving my car to walk in the direction of a main thoroughfare to look for help. I had no snow boots for protection on my trek so I returned to my car. In those very late hours I had to be content to run the engine and heater until daybreak.

About daybreak I was pulled free to reach the cleared roads. When I reached Opsal's the news was that we had broken records for late season snowfall. Later that morning I made my way to Sears to wait in line to buy tire chains and have them installed. It would be days before the snow would be cleared and a past due warm spell would start to melt the rest. I was so disgusted I left the chains on my station wagon until I felt there was no way I could get stuck. It was a bad week to accomplish any productive work and I am sure my mind was working overtime to find my way out of this place.

When I returned to Minneapolis the year before, I had bought a new station wagon for a work truck. My futile attempt to work the station wagon out of the snow caused the engine to overheat. I drove over to the car dealer for a check up. I was told that the valves had been burned. The mechanic suggested I do nothing and since the noise was hardly noticeable I should trade it in for another car. Right then I was in no mood to do anything but finish the work I was committed to. Within a few days I made up my mind, in June I would leave for California. I would tell no one..

Several weeks later, when spring made its full arrival, I spotted a real gem that would get me out of Minneapolis. At Malkerson Oldsmobile showroom was a beautiful yellow convertible with a dark green top. Convertibles in Minnesota make about as much sense as owning a beach umbrella. A salesman who was eager to move this misplaced beast made a very acceptable offer in which I would trade my station wagon. Now I had my final reason to leave for California. Now everyone knew, my days were numbered. My good-byes were short and final.

As I headed west from Minneapolis, I took the same route as in March 1951. But when I reached South Dakota, I went straight west through the Black Hills. I would pass through a town called Yankton, South Dakota. It was a reminder of my childhood days on the farm

and the 'honky tonk' lyrics of Lulu Belle and Scotie. Their folksy music was transmitted from Yankton. It was the first time I drove through Yellowstone Park. The place glowed with beauty in the warm early summer sun. The place lived up to its many praises including the bears begging along the roadsides.

Those were still innocent times in America back then. There were no freeways. Every road was a country road and before the cars traversed them, they were used by the horse pulled wagons. There was no crowd in Yellowstone Park. As I made the all-day loop it was as though I had this majestic spot to myself. At that time I was intrigued with the rustic and near empty camp grounds. What a great place to camp I thought. Interestingly the next time I came this way would be in 1961 in a Volkswagen camper. Traveling with me was my wife, Jeanne, and our two small daughters Laura and Claire. This time the bears had names like 'Yogi'.

That night I stayed in the park in an uncrowned Yellowstone Lodge. It was a sort of celebration that my long delayed trip to California was happening. The next day I traveled the old highway through Star Valley and into Ogden, a place I left only 20 months before. How long ago it felt! As the next few days slipped by my thoughts wandered as to what I would do when I reached California to start a new life. I had all my tools in the trunk and I didn't have the slightest idea what was in store.

It was Sunday when I arrived in Los Angeles at my Uncle Bill and Aunt Lorraine's house. I had a different feeling of hope and excitement than I had over three years before when I arrived to enter Birmingham hospital. They were happy to see me and how well I had recovered.

The next morning at breakfast Uncle Bill was reading the job ads and told me that Hughes Aircraft was hiring. At this time the Korean war was still ongoing. Hughes was only three miles away and was busily developing the first air to air guided missiles and airborne radar systems. He said construction was far out in the suburbs and the thousands of cheap tract homes were a formidable competitor to private contractors. He was right.

After breakfast I got dressed in my casual best along with my credentials of past aircraft experience and headed for Hughes. After a job application was filled out I was directed to a department for an interview in the field test section. I was introduced to Bill Birkholz and to Jim Beck. Within short minutes I had a very good job and was sent back to personnel for processing to come to work immediately.

After a lengthy process of completing numerous papers, because this was a defense contractor, I was directed to an office to complete the final papers. Sitting behind the desk was one beautiful lady, about my age, with an Irish complexion and sparkling auburn hair. Her name was Beverly Bookout. As she made herself busy with signing papers, she was also asking many personal questions beyond the norms of employment. At the end of the session she asked me, "Would you like to come for dinner at my place tonight?" Of course, the answer was yes.

I had hardly been in Los Angeles for one day and I had a place to stay, a good job and a beautiful new girlfriend. California was great.

Life is made up of a collection of things that can be little building blocks or giant milestones. I would find that Minnesota was a place of little building blocks and of limited horizons. On the other hand, California was a fast growing place that had little time for pettiness of ethnicity, ones roots or family standing. It was a state on the roll, for good or bad. But it was a place to build careers. I would never regret leaving Minnesota.

My natural gift of creating things I could build would for now be a part time hobby for five years. The heavy population growth produced a new industry called 'tract housing'. One developer by the name of

Mr. Pointe was possibly the champion of price, quantity and high production homes in the 50s. His homes covered untold acres of once productive orchard and farm land with affordable look-alike homes. These homes were so plentiful that they were nearly all 'no money down' opportunities.

My new job and a vast improvement in my handicaps gave me a new excitement for life. My biggest worry was getting up in time for work. Los Angeles was a huge place that would take me time to find my way around. It was not long before I knew where I would like to live, but the cost was beyond my ability to pay. For now it was time for me to enjoy the 'American Dream'. And I did just that.

When I arrived in California it was a place that not only boasted a life style of freedom, but opportunity where business thrived and things were affordable. It was a place where new aircraft were produced for war and peace. Technology was moving so fast that these machines were obsolete even before they were tested. A new technical age was developing fast to face our newest enemy, Russia. The growth of California was so intense it would one day be the most populous state.

The car was king and if the one you owned was older than two years there was something wrong with your value system. There were drive-in movies and hamburger stands. California was a safe place and you could travel wherever you wanted. Everything was here. There were miles of empty beaches and only a short ride to camping in magnificent pine and redwood forests.

California did everything best. The music business was professional and the best were rewarded well. It was the days of the Beach Boys, The Lettermen, and The Freshmen. Rosemary Clooney and other sound-alikes were selling big. By now Jo Stafford's big hit "You Belong To Me" was old news but its soulful message of world travel tugged in my restless spirit. Back then musicians and vocalists had talent and the music world was upbeat and exciting. The trashy pop music of today would never find an audience in this demanding time of America. It was a kinder and more civilized time. The family was something to love and provide for and nothing was too good for them. I am glad I was a part of it.

California was a romantic and prolific place. The servicemen who had experienced California while deployed here during the war knew it was better than the cold shabby states of their birthplaces. They couldn't build schools fast enough to educate the baby boomers. I too joined the parade and married Jeanne in March of 1955. My old flame Beverly Bookout had become a casualty of my overprotective landlords, Lynn and Bill, who were certain that their good friend would be a better choice for me than Beverly Bookout. Soon I would be part of the new California culture of a new tract house, wife, two kids, dogs, high fidelity music system, and a back yard with cement block fences, swimming pool and monthly payments on everything.

Jeanne was born in Los Angeles, 28 August 1925. Born into a family of Jewish heritage, she would not be easily accepted by my family who considered roots as important. She was well-educated and was graduated from UCLA with a degree in music and English. She studied voice and, when I met her, she was entertaining in clubs. She also worked in Hollywood for KHJ radio as a music programmer who enjoyed a mix with the Hollywood subculture. Jeanne was a very serious and sober person who could hardly be aligned with a simple farm boy with an unknown future as an M.S. victim.

Jeanne Vivatson

Bill, Jeanne and baby Laura in March, 1956

There is no cure for Multiple Sclerosis to this day. The disease attacks the insulation of the nervous system. Its first strike leaves a variety of near permanent damages behind. A marginal recovery can last up to five to ten years when it will strike again with more devastating losses. This interim time is called remission. For whatever reasons be it love, infatuation, hormones or dedication, she chose to marry me, knowing full well that one day she would carry my burdens. It is now over 50 years later and only she can tell you if it was worth the gamble.

Back then the workplace was dominated with transplants from all over the country. This population shift caused people to count on friends for socializing in the absence of relatives. The work place would be where people would make life long acquaintances. It was so in the case of our family.

Baby Laura, Jeanne and grandma, Claire Acton

Through the years we became close to the Krebs, the Fords, the Cimorellis, the Moloskis, the Millers and many others. Even today we share Christmas greetings with those who are still with us.

Interestingly, many of our friends would be a source for practicing my skills of drawing plans and helping with remodel projects. I had a good job and many of these free projects would be a time of learning the California way of doing things. I would even do some practicing on the two tract houses we owned.

March 1960, Bill with Claire and Laura in Granada Hills

By 1958, the California economy ran out of gas. A military man made president lived up to his promise and ended the Korean War. After this was settled, he attempted to be an economist and the defense industry tumbled. By this time Mr. Eisenhower would rather play golf than mind business, and soon California was in a deep recession. It took years for California to recover.

My job was in jeopardy several times as the defense industry was struggling to live on less. It would be the generous hand of Mr. King and Frank Morris that would shuffle paper and positions to save my employment with them.

Money was scarce and I needed something to do in my spare time. Word got around that if it were made from wood or cement I could build it. The California life style was rewriting how people lived and the backyard was becoming the family haven. The day of backyard swimming pools had arrived and become as cheap as a bottom of the line car. We had to have one too. And following the pool, was the covered patio. I would build dozens of these structures and it was a chance to be inspired to come up with new ideas. My remodeling plans became great practice opportunities and I would learn the local building codes.

By 1962 I had a dream of moving on up to the right side of the tracks. Our second tract house was planted in a walnut grove and I was completely fed up with tract house mentality. Too many people that purchased these cheap tract homes should have stayed in apartments. Too many tracts were becoming slums. At the time we were living in the north San Fernando Valley area and my eyes coveted the property of the south side of Ventura Boulevard. It was the place of magical communities called Encino, Sherman Oaks, Studio City, Tarzana and Woodland Hills — a place I wanted to be.

We had a little money saved, but we would have to sell our existing home in a weak market. In our spare time we would cruise these areas for the right property but mostly we were in a dream world being tempted with the taste of 'forbidden fruit'. In the process of our search we drove slowly up and down strange streets copying down realtors numbers on for sale signs.

It was during these long days of a California recession I spent evenings reading about my dreams of world travel. I doubt if I ever thought it would happen to the extent of my curiosity but I kept reading. To spare disappointment, my dreams were kept to myself. The TV still had little interest for me and I was content with books and dreams. One of my favorite publications was the *National Geographic*. It was the time that the very young (17) Robin Graham set out with his sailboat *Dove* on an around the world journey. As I read the articles that appeared over many months of his journey, my childhood dream took root. As I sized up his small 26-foot boat of marginal strength, I was convinced it was a possible dream. I always thought a single trip to the Hawaiian Islands was what I wanted to make. For now it was a silent dream.

One day our dreams took a new turn as our house was sold to the right person at a fair price. The next good fortune would be to locate a lot that had recently come on the market by an out-of-state owner, an airline pilot. It was a two-third acre plot in the right neighborhood. It was in the Tarzana area and part of the Edward Rice Burrows' estate, the creator of *Tarzan*. Our offer was accepted and we owned a beautiful lot on the right side of the tracks. There was a lesson to be learned in our new purchase. That is, never be in a big hurry when making serious plans for your future. Of course it helps to have a 'money-wise' wife.

It was a neighborhood of fine homes, new and old, with huge mature trees everywhere. I would be happy just living here in a tent. It was a place dreams are made of.

We started construction in 1963. It was a do-it-yourself project including the plans. The only carpenters and painters on the job were my wife and I. These were more simple times and local government was more tolerant of owner builders. The main house would finish first and a rock bordered swimming pool would be next. A large guest house was built for my wife's mother.

A dream was realized and we now lived on the right side of the boulevard. We were broke, but my dream was realized. There was an inherent glitch in my nature that compelled me to put my best foot forward. No doubt it was the abject poverty of life on the prairie that drove me to do better. I was never a person to be content to stand still, and change was my motivator. It was also an energy I carried into old age.

There were many things I would be driven to do that were like blind compulsions. After the challenge was achieved I would find out that new doors would open. The open doors would be long reaching opportunities that would never have happened if I had not heeded my ambition to build our own home. Our new home was such a stepping stone. It was also a statement of what I could do. It also caused me to learn some very important lessons by my mistakes that I would not make a second time.

I have long ago found out that when one makes a wise choice it is an invitation for another good idea to present itself. Our choice of a large agricultural property would become a place for me to have a cabinet shop. The long lasting recession would never be a problem for me. There was an endless list of customers waiting for my handiwork.

My obsession to be south of the boulevard would only last for seven years and we moved on. But wherever we would later go we had stability because of my wife. Very quickly after we were married she gave up her career and willingly invested her time in a soon growing family. She was a woman without an agenda of her own and chose to make us, Laura, Claire and myself, her personal responsibility.

Her determination and instinctive nature of common sense made our move across the tracks and our new home possible. Her family enjoyed a home of comfort, order and stability. It was her gracious

Claire Acton

manner that always made our home a welcome place for others. This was an important asset for one who would eventually be in the business of designing and building dream houses. Of course she was equally adept at planning a two-week camping trip in a Volkswagen minibus for the whole family including the dogs.

Soon there would be doors open in my life I could never permit myself to even dream about. It was as though my new extended family set a stage whereby others could feel safe investing in my life. My career was a legend caused and made by others. This too, Jeanne made possible. To know where these qualities came from, you would have to meet her mother.

Claire Acton was a descendant of Jewish immigrants who left Hungary a century ago. Her father escaped by using a horse's passport that took him first to South America and then America. She was a person of great talent and class. In her younger years, during the 'roaring twenties,' she was a club singer with a large following. She was a featured entertainer of the once opulent gambling ship that was anchored offshore from Los Angeles.

During the Great Depression she lost her husband and all alone she raised her two daughters through these troubled years. Mrs. Acton accomplished this feat by opening an attractive women's clothing store in very hard times. She was a person who was respected by customers and friends alike. The success in that one store would permit her one day to move from a small cottage in Venice to a beautiful place across the tracks to Brentwood. It was a reward for a person who knew no compromise.

Her leap was a more formidable one. She would buy, in 1949, a new model home that she and her family would enjoy for years. It was a home that had been featured in *Architectural Digest* — a magnificent home with the heavy wood look that inspired me to do my best. But for Claire Acton it was a house of hospitality. It was the home where I would ask her if I could marry her daughter. It was her home where her daughter and I were married.

The word 'generosity' was best defined by the person of Claire Acton. One of her many quotations were, "Don't give someone the shirt off your back, buy them a new one!" The critical word 'cheap' would never symbolize Claire Acton. There was a long duration of time that when I would dress up, everything I wore, except the shoes, were gifts from her. Her taste was always the best and would represent the best in my closet.

I enjoyed the privileged status of 'favorite son'. Every Wednesday night we were at Grandma's house for dinner. She was an excellent cook and what was served was always my favorite. One Wednesday evening it was necessary for my wife to scold her for only preparing my favorite dishes.

She was a professional with good business sense. It wasn't easy to keep a store open for decades and keep a loyal clientele. But for Mrs. Acton, like all of us mortals, life was slipping by and she wanted to fulfill a life's dream and open a new restaurant. Her new dream would soon fall victim to an unprofessional and unscrupulous contractor who consumed her finances and valuable time. Her gift of being a good cook would not necessarily translate into a profitable restaurant and instead became a heavy burden to carry.

In the end she would be troubled with debt and failing health and forced to call it time to quit. She worked hard and long and now failing health was making all the decisions for her.

She had great interest in our building project and would bring out huge lunches to the construction site. My respect and love for her made it easy for me to ask if she would come and live with us. The plan would be to build a guest house for her overlooking the pool. She agreed but one day in the not too distant future she would be taken to the hospital. Her long years of stress and mostly caring for the troubles of others took their final toll. She would leave us and be painfully missed.

Mrs. Acton was a person that would be a living example in my life. Her life was a celebration of the best the human can achieve. She was a class act.

Memorable quotes by Claire Acton

About partnerships, "Never own a yellow dog with anyone."

A disorganized social event, "A Jewish picnic."

On guest manners, "You might as well eat, because I am going to tell every one you ate dinner here."

On finances, "Never do business with relatives."

On political fairness, "It all depends on whose ox is being gored."

On trust, "Never give anyone a stick to hit you with."

About complaining customers, "Never argue with a customer, just give his money back and you will save yourself a customer."

About a bad marriage, "There are worse things in life than living alone."

When I search my memory it reveals a collage of incidents that make the story of my life more insignificant and rather it is the impact of the lives of others in my life that becomes more important. One of

Auntie Florine Warmoth

those persons was a relative of my wife called Florine Warmoth. She had lost her husband years before and had recently retired from AT&T. Although she was only cousin status to Mrs. Acton she enjoyed a relationship more like her sister. And to us, she bridged the role between an auntie and grandmother to our children. Florine would fill a huge void in our lives for decades.

One time when Florine came to visit us with her welcome gift of comfort, we were reflecting on our loss and our unfulfilled plans for Mrs. Acton to live with us. During this visit I would reflect on the qualities of this person called Florine and I instinctively knew I wanted her in my family's lives and asked her if she would live with us in the guest house.

Florine was a wise woman and cautiously said, "Why don't we both think it over for a couple of weeks." The time passed and we were all in agreement. She moved into the guest house in 1964. Florine was a grandmother of epic proportions. The guest house was at least seventy feet from the house but our young daughters and the two dogs had a deeply worn path to her house. It was a relationship few would ever understand. Once a relative remarked to me as to how I could live around a relative. My answer was, "Florine has been a blessing and I would have it no other way."

Florine's generosity to my wife, our children and myself could only be compared to one's own mother and father. For our children she would be the kindest grandmother, the best baby sitter and their closest friend. Her door of welcome was always open and if you entered her door there was an immediate offer of something to eat or drink. Every Friday night for years our family was her guest to enjoy dinner at a fine restaurant.

If my wife and I planned a trip, Florine was the only baby sitter that would be needed, and she was the best. We were a camping family and Florine had her first introduction to this wilderness experience with us. She was soon involved and shared the 'roughing it' life style just like the kids. It was unthinkable for our family to plan a camping trip without her. Some of our trips would be a couple thousand miles long and she would be there, in the back of the small camper with the kids and dogs and loving it.

As my career as a builder developed my family and I made many moves, but Florine would always come with us without a complaint. She was a real blessing to my family.

CHAPTER EIGHT
My Day Had Arrived

It was 1966 and the economy in California was still in the basement. Too many people were moving to California and less military spending kept wages down. To add to the nation's problems, the 'Hippie Movement' became bigger than life. It was started by rebellious young men who were the children of the 'greatest generation', the WWII heroes who gave us freedom. As these pampered boys screamed to protest social injustice they left behind a path of deadly riots, murder, burned out buildings and whatever else they could destroy. They moved about in smelly Volkswagen minibuses and were emboldened with drugs and outrageous behavior. Soon the foolish young women would join this gang of misfits and it was called the 'sexual revolution'. This new breed of outlaws was cheered on with a new kind of music and musicians who wailed a message of hatred of America. Some of these were Bob Dylan, Jonie Mitchel, Joan Baez, Cat Stevens and the Beatles.

Before long, the unpopular Viet Nam War would broaden their agenda and numbers, and our nation was being divided and crippled.

1968 back packing trip with daughter Laura on the Sierra John Muir trail to Mt. Whitney

*Daughters Laura and Claire on a back packing trip in the
Sequoia National Forest with the author in 1970*

It was the end of a once unified patriotic America. Tragically it ushered in a new era when new values accepted that, "Evil is good, and good is evil."

Life in our new home on the right side of the tracks was wonderful but we were cash poor. I was thankful to have my job at Martin Marietta but wished I had more part-time construction work.

At 41 years of age I was getting serious about making something happen. My restless nature needed some sort of an outlet for exercise and mental stimulation. My choice would be the Sierra Hiking Club because it was the cheapest hobby I could think of. It required little investment and the outdoor wilderness was a place I loved. I took my young daughters on some trips but it was the older, Laura, who took the most interest in this strenuous hobby. Together we had hiked two of the three sections of the John Muir trail, including a hike to the top of Mr. Whitney. One late October I joined a group of Sierra Club hikers in San Francisco area. It was a week long hike on the John Muir trail south of Tahoe. They were all professionals, educators and medical people. Our leader was a geologist. All were very cool and well endowed with self importance. The last night of our wonderful hike, we were gathered around a big fire taking turns sharing what we wanted to accomplish in our lifetime. I felt out of place and wished I could have slipped away. My accomplishments, I thought, were insignificant compared to this crowd. Of course I spoke last. Prophetically, my response went like this. I said that I wanted to retire by age 50 so that I could travel or do whatever I wanted. Someone questioned me as how I intended to make this happen. My reply, I wanted to build rental property for income. It was this idea that permitted us to retire at age 51.

Truthfully I had harbored some regret that I only had a high school education. And perhaps I did envy those with college educations and jobs with exciting titles and personalized parking spaces. But I never felt I was too good to work at whatever was available. My final decision to attempt to reach prospective customers was to print business cards that would list what I could do. I distributed my cards to people who lived south of the boulevard. Hopefully they had the money to give me jobs. My cards read like a shopping list of carpentry.

Saturday morning I got dressed up in casual clothes and headed for Ventura Boulevard to distribute my new cards. Ventura Boulevard runs

At the time of this photo, the author was walking Ventura Boulevard handing out business cards to shop keepers. Shortly after one of his cards fell into the hands of Al and Ceil Podell and forever his life would be changed.

from its westerly limits of Woodland Hills to North Hollywood. It was a distance of ten miles. I chose to walk the boulevard in the direction of North Hollywood. This would be the communities of Tarzana, Encino and Sherman Oaks.

Ventura Boulevard was well populated with upscale restaurants and numerous shops for carpeting, drapes, furniture, art galleries and interior decorators. When I entered each store I always asked for the owner or manager. I introduced myself and explained what I could do. I was always well received. If I thought there was an expensive looking residential area I left the boulevard and knocked on doors. Everyone took my card.

It was a long day. I felt that more cards should be handed out so I coerced my family to drive into different neighborhoods and give the cards to homeowners. My modest family would instead stick my cards into mailboxes. For sure I got one response, a letter from the post office.

I didn't have to wait long for my first customer. It was a carpet company calling me to cut the bottoms of doors to clear the new long shag carpeting that had become the latest California fad. I must have cut off hundreds of doors.

As I became busier it was obvious that my old power tools were not up to the job. A few months later I received a call from a doctor who was remodeling a large old house in Sherman Oaks. His project was ready for cabinets and he showed me what he would need. I knew that my marginal Sears power tools would never produce what he wanted. Cautiously I told him to let me build a few of the cabinets and see if they met his satisfaction.

When I went home I told my wife about my job offer and that I should have better tools. I suggested I should look for some used professional tools in order to make decent cabinets. She suggested I buy new. I wouldn't argue that offer and my shopping spree would be the cost of a cheap new car.

The first cabinets were accepted by a satisfied customer and I did the entire job. This single job made a huge contribution to my new tool investment. Decades later these tools are still in my possession.

I have to be honest about the reasons I wanted to buy property south of the boulevard. Plain and simple, it was vanity. However in a few years I knew the benefits were far beyond my expectations. The operation of a cabinet shop is noisy. Our large property permitted enough distance between homes to absorb the tool noise. Eventually I soundproofed my garage and for all the years we lived there our neighbors never complained.

Opportunities that can change lives come in all sorts of packages. For me, it was that Saturday walk to distribute some simple business cards that would change my life. At the time I was 41 years old and I retired at age 51! But most important it was these 10 short years that saw the fruition of my childhood dreams come to be. It was also the time that my natural gift of creativity would be established and my career as an architect and builder would be realized. My testimony embraces a simple cliché, 'You have not because you do not ask'. Come with me and meet the people who miraculously opened the doors to a new career, mine.

My day had arrived with a call from Al Podell who lived in Encino. His phone call was to inquire if I could remodel his laundry room. I told him the job was something I could do and we set up a time to meet. In a few days we met and discussed the job. A price was agreed on and I was on my way.

The job was completed on time and he had another project for me. At this time he told me that his children were all grown and had left home and he and his wife Ceil decided it was time to remodel and redecorate their very large but older home.

Before long Mr. Podell simply told me to do the job and give him the bill when finished. Eventually he trusted me with the building and installation of large built-in cabinets and bookcases made of walnut for his study. I worked for him on different projects for about two years. It was some time before I knew that Mr. Podell was the sole owner of the state wide Cal Auto Store chain. He was a very prosperous man but more importantly a very able business man. I listened closely to his financial and business advice. I felt very comfortable with him and his wife Ceil. They had invited us out for dinner and to their home to discuss ongoing projects. I knew he had placed considerable trust in me and I appreciated this.

As my world was turning faster I was reminded of my mortality with the return of my arrhythmia. I required a simple surgery procedure that required general anesthesia. What was to be routine would have me awakening in a sitting position in a hospital bed being slapped around by a medical staff. When I awoke a very, very angry surgeon

Ceil and Al Podell

demanded of me, "Why didn't you tell us you had arrhythmia. You went into shock." I went to a heart specialist and was given an open prescription for Valium and back on full schedule.

Time was slipping by and it was now well into 1968. My building work had become so successful that I was earning more from it than my full-time job. By now we had invested in a beach lot in the Pierpont Beach community in Ventura. I drew up plans for a two story duplex. The project was completed and sold in September of 1969. Emboldened by our success, we purchased another beach lot and also a lot in the Ventura Keys on the ocean-access canal for our next dream house.

About this time we invited Al and Ceil Podell to our Tarzana home for dinner. They had never been in our home before. I know they were pleasantly surprised with our home and possibly had a different perspective of my ability. But I am only guessing. We discussed our projects and our plans for our future. By now we had placed our present home on the market as we made plans to move to Ventura. It was an interesting evening as we all discussed things we had heretofore never thought of sharing and got to know each other better.

Soon after I had another project from Mr. Podell and it was at this time that he made me an offer. It was that we should build an apartment building together. The arrangement would be that I would find a lot, do the plans and supervise the construction and he would put up all the front money. After completion, a loan would be placed on the property and we would become equal partners. The significance of the offer would change my life. For sure I would never have received such an offer if I was a California 'hippie'.

My work went on but the new excitement for building an apartment project with the Podells' inspired me to get busy and look for a lot. My interest was no longer in Tarzana so I started looking at the Ventura Beach area. My search soon had me looking at two pieces of property on Harbor Boulevard at the entrance to the Ventura Keyes marina. The two lots were heavily landscaped with large slump stone walls and huge gas lanterns that graced the entrance. I was disappointed when my realtor, Al Barlow, informed me that the property was dedicated to the Ventura Keys Association.

For now I accepted his explanation. But a short time later when I was in the title office I checked and found that the property belonged to Pacesetter Homes in Laguna Beach. They were the developers of the marina community and canals. I got back to Mr. Barlow and told him of my discovery and if he would check and see if they would sell the lots. In only a day, Al Barlow called and told me they would sell and he stated the price. Within days, Al and Ceil Podell had invested in my career with the purchase of property in the Ventura Keys.

There would be three lots in all. One on the southerly corner and the other two would be to the north of the entrance. Restrictive zoning established by the development of the Ventura Keyes limited the lots to three apartment units each with two parking spaces. The two northerly lots if joined would permit twelve units if regular Ventura city planning laws were applied. I went to the Ventura city planning department and asked if it were possible to request permission to; 1. Join the two lots into one. 2. Permit twelve units rather than six. 3. Permit tandem parking to accommodate two parking spaces per unit. They agreed I would be permitted a hearing. I would have to submit working drawings — a copy for each of the ten council members and several for the office. The owners were expected to appear with their agent.

I had a full plate and loved every minute. My architectural skills were something I had picked up as a hobby. I had also taken a couple night semester classes on perspective drawing. My drafting equipment was a piece of plywood, T-square and a few basics. From the day I knew the lots were available my sketch pad had been busy. I decided on a twelve-unit complex, two stories high, fashioned around an open court. An existing alley made a parking carport practical. Nearly all the units were two bedrooms and two baths with fireplaces. The design of the building would be heavy Spanish with heavy lumber, wrought iron and tile roof. The structure has for years been a very visible landmark.

My drawing project took a couple months. I harbored fears that my drawings would be too amateurish but I did not want to spend unnecessary money on an architect. I had figured out long ago that good room proportion was the secret to good design. I tried to make each apartment look more like a home rather than the typical box apartment.

Before long the rolls of prints and application for the zoning variance hearing were in the hands of the Ventura Planning Department. After a quick review of the documents they assigned me a hearing date. As the date drew near I called Mr. Podell to remind him when to join me in Ventura for the hearing. He advised me to go by myself because he would only look like a Los Angeles investor. It passed my mind that I might be a little presumptuous appearing by myself. Normally a project like this would have a polished architect make the presentation. But instead a rank novice would be making the pitch.

On the day of the hearing it was a regular work day for me. I was up at 6:00 A.M. and the hearing was to be in the evening at 7:00 P.M. I knew that about the only thing I had going for myself was to be well dressed. I wore my light blue suit with dark blue tie. I arrived on time with my set of drawings and a copy of a perspective of the project. The printed agenda showed three other cases before me, I would be last.

The three petitioners ahead of me dragged on. I was tired and I was ready. Everything I could do was complete, even the rehearsing of my presentation. It must have been well after eight before my turn came.

My presentation was robotic and concise. My primary focus would be on the looks of the building and the large size of the units. I emphasized the wide and large tandem parking spaces that were well off the access alley. There were few questions. There was a short and quiet discussion between the council members. Then very quickly the president said, "Mr. Vivatson your project is approved unanimously." I thanked them.

As I started to remove my drawings from the easels there was the noisy shuffling of chairs and people talking. One of the council women came up to me with a big smile. She touched my arm and said, "Mr. Vivatson, with that blue outfit and those blue eyes did you think for a minute that your project wouldn't be approved?" I was speechless but offered her a thank you.

On the long ride back to Tarzana I felt relaxed and victorious. It was a wonderful achievement and I was anxious to get home and call Mr. Podell.

My next step would be to find an engineer/architect that would engineer my plans. It was not long before I was referred to Andy Stevenson. Andy was a kindly professional that was happy to check my plans. And for years he would be stamping everything I designed. How fortunate I was, I had a professional I could count on. One of the nicest compliments that I would ever receive came from Andy. One day be asked me, "Bill, where do you come up with all these ideas?" Right now it is years later and I honestly don't know.

A short time later I received a call from Al Barlow asking me to stop by the office. When I arrived he informed me that the Golden Builders had told him that if I started the apartment without a licensed contractor they would report me to the California Contractors Board. I wasn't surprised because they had their eye on me. They were the most active builders on the beach and they must have viewed me as a threat. Once they said of me, "How can you compete against a cabinet-maker building a house."

I never worked with a contractor so I had few options. I decided to call Mel Zuravin who was a general contractor. Our friendship came about because he and his wife had two daughters the same age as ours and they were in the same school. We got to know each other well while driving our children back and forth. My request brought a quick response from Mel to tell me to pick up and fill out the forms and to make arrangements for a bond and he would sign it. It would be a few weeks and I was a licensed California State Contractor.

I could not help but think that in the past few months there were three men who would open all the doors for my new career as an architect and builder. First, it would be Al Podell who supplied the financing for the development of the apartments at the entrance to the Ventura Keyes. They would be showplaces for my skills. Second, it was Andy Stevenson who supplied his talent to engineer my buildings and give me advice. And third, it was Mel Zuravin who provided me with a contractor's license. At the time I was interested to realize that both Mr. Podell and Mel Zuravin were Jewish. Later, I would understand why this was to be..

I would be remiss if I did not thank Ed Nafe, a principal of Golden Builders, for causing me to get my contractors license. I would have been more than content to stay with my profitable cabinet shop.

The twelve units were finished by mid-1971. The project was a success and later that year the Ventura City Planning Department approved a plan to place a five unit apartment on the southerly corner. Later the same year our new dream house would be built on the Ventura Keyes canal and we moved in and became Ventura residents. The same year I quit my job at Martin Marietta. This huge conglomerate even contributed to my creative skills.

I had been with Martin Marietta for over ten years. My years with the company were time well spent. My two supervisors, Mr. Morris and Hal Stevenson gave me many opportunities to learn and use my ideas. At that time they developed and produced the navigation computers for the Polaris Submarine. There was a time that the access doors on all the computers were my design. On my last day of work it was not easy to say good-bye. I had great respect for that company and the security, opportunity and favor they gave me.

It was 1972 and my day had arrived. People came to me to design and build their homes. For the next six years my life would be a whirlwind of productive activity. I would forever willingly share my success with those who caused it all to happen.

But in a very few years this successful part of our lives would end, and a totally new direction would bring about changes we could never have imagined — changes that would again test our abilities to adapt to a new and uncharted future.

CHAPTER NINE

Appointed Architect
and Builder

It was 1972 and the doors of opportunity were open for Bill Vivatson. Al and Ceil Podell had made it possible to build the two Spanish apartment buildings that impressively stood at the entry gate to the Ventura Keys Marina. Although I never placed my name on them during or after construction I was already known as the architect and builder.

About two blocks away in the Ventura Keys stood our new home. It was also done in a Spanish motif. The presence of these three new buildings would immediately act as a shingle to boast the 'new kid' on the block.

Even before the completion of our new home our postman, Dick Eckstrom, became very interested in our new project. One day he told me that he owned a beach lot and asked if I would design a new home for him and his wife. Spanish was synonymous with Ventura but it also made a very showy building whether you liked it or not. The new home of the Eckstroms made a strong statement on the beach and work came in faster than I could produce.

There was a man by the name of Robert Armstrong who contributed mightily to my ability to build the many structures I had designed in the Ventura area. He had framed the twelve and five unit apartments.

Robert's talent made him one of the most capable framers of large and complicated commercial buildings like waterfront restaurants. After he framed the twelve unit apartment, he was working on a large building and fell off a ladder with a skill saw in his hand. It was a terrible accident that would result in full recovery, but bad memories lingered. He no longer wanted to be involved with large commercial structures. This was my gain.

For the next six years he worked nearly full time for me on my projects. My gift of creativity was not stuck on the popular Spanish but almost any style the customer could want. It was the talented and proficient Robert who would compliment my buildings. We were professional friends with never a conflict. He made it all possible.

My small beach houses and duplexes were popping up like weeds until a break came that let me design an oceanfront home. Don Carlton, Al Barlow's broker, was the most active realtor in the beach community. One evening he called me and suggested I call Mr. and Mrs. Douglas Beidebach as they were looking for an architect. Mr. Beidebach was an executive for Moores Business Forms and had just been transferred to Ventura. Douglas and his wife Susan had just purchased an oceanfront lot and would need someone to design and build their new home.

At our first meeting when their new home was being discussed Susan was quick to mention that they did not like Spanish. She told me they liked the heavy wood beach look. They had two small children and a list of things they wanted in their new home. I left with their wish list after suggesting some ideas on sketch paper. I said I would have something in a week.

Oceanfront home of Susan and Douglas Biedebach

My first oceanfront house at Pierpont was three stories high. The first level garage was dug into the sand dune with the living area above. The exterior was all solid cedar and black glass. Facing the ocean was a mezzanine study that overlooked the living room with a lofted ceiling.

The oceanfront side was a long two story structure with a full portico placed well off the sand. It was supported with an impressive row of cedar columns each about a foot square. The front entry on the inland side had the same look with a glassed in stairway. It instantly earned the name, 'the Long House'. Over the years when people asked me where I got my ideas I would always answer, "Nothing is new."

Two years later there was a terrible explosion, caused by a gas main rupture that totally destroyed the structure. The Beidebachs insisted that the insurance company hire me to replace the structure exactly as it was before. They were great contributors to my success on the beach.

The story I am about to share will most likely sound like a sales pitch for my exceptional talent, but it is not. As I attempt to reflect, 30 years later, on all the structures I designed and built in these seven years it seems almost impossible. There are few reasons that could justify my rapid climb as an architect and builder. I was a rank novice. Unquestionably there was a latent creative gift that had been pent up since childhood. I might consider that my roots of poverty or handicap would cause me to grab at an opportunity when I recognized it.

But I think there is a more serious answer. I believe very strongly that there is a purpose for our lives. However, it is not always at the time we choose. Or was it possible that He could not trust me with my talent and an architect's credential? It is only in the past years that I have come to believe the loss of my eyesight at a critical time of my life was intended to induce humility. Possibly I may never know. And after all, there are all those I have to thank for making it all possible in spite of my handicaps.

The homes were produced as fast as Robert could frame them. Before long I knew who the best subcontractors were and we developed faithful relationships that made for satisfied customers. My subcontractors were never chosen on the basis of price. There were about five of my subcontractors that had me design and build their homes. My relationship with lenders and bankers were all fast track loans. I was exempt from the need of filling out long tedious specification forms like most other builders. I eventually had the respect of bankers whereby they would declare, "If Vivatson is building your home just give him your checkbook."

Historically the 'contractor culture' well earned their negative reputation of untrustworthiness. It is the same culture as the professional salesman. That is, promise one thing and deliver something else. I grew up in a family where honesty and our word meant everything. And also, as people who lived through the Great Depression we understood the value of honesty because we were poor. Another principle I learned was to always keep my own fees low. I always wanted my clients to feel I was a 'bargain'.

I am sure I never felt I was pressured but rather I enjoyed the excitement of having a 'full plate'. I designed every structure I built. The biggest problem I had was to have enough private time to draw. Many of us have a preconceived idea that the design of a new home starts in an air-conditioned office with a huge drafting table with a mechanical arm. Stacked around the office are impressive engineering manuals and catalogs. It was not so with me. My private office would be a new Ericson 29 sloop. My childhood dream of owning a sailboat was possible and would have a dual purpose. For me it was a fun hobby and sailing was now my new pastime. The sailboat became the perfect office. The roomy bright cabin was a perfect place to draw. No one could come into the marina without a key and there was no phone.

As the demand for my services rapidly increased, I was forced to become more efficient. I am certain that my sight handicap forced me to be more resourceful. The design of a new home can become very time consuming and tedious unless one is able to make decisions quickly. I never permitted a client to bring a box full of magazine clippings of ideas for their new home. They could only bring two pictures of an exterior and the same for each room. Next, I believed that a home must be attractive and interesting. Therefore 'form' had preference over 'function'. I designed an interesting house and made the rooms fit.

Possibly the most important design principle I used was this; After both the client and I agreed on everything the new home was to be I told them I would draw only one design, I did not design by trial and error. It worked every time.

There is a magic in loving what one does for a living. I had found my place. I had found my talent and gift and it was the golden moment of my life. I did not live the mold of a gifted architect but rather I was a person who lived to please people. My rewards followed that commitment.

I don't want to give the impression that my life was all work. I would never hesitate to work seven days a week but I knew when we should get away. I had equipped my sailboat for single handed sailing with the help of an electric autopilot. It was an exciting time in my life. I was fortunate that Jeanne was an excellent property manager and bookkeeper. I think our greatest family fun was eating out at one of the numerous good restaurants in Ventura.

In late 1972 we purchased a lot on the sand dunes of the Pierpont Beach. Most of my clients were building beach homes and I decided we should be part of them. It was a three-story structure of heavy timbers, shakes, shingles, and used brick. It had a tough, New England beach look. Once again I would drag my uncomplaining family to a new street address.

I was extremely fortunate that as my business grew I attracted a certain clientele who wanted a custom home that would look good. Possibly it was the looks of my building that discouraged a tight-budget customer from ever calling me. By 1973 most of my customers were doctors or professionals. And like my early times in St. Louis Park, Minnesota, many were Jewish. For whatever reason, I had not yet understood why.

In 1973, Mr. John Maitland and his wife Carmel purchased an ocean-front lot in Pierpont Beach. John was the president of MCA Corporation and the vice president for Universal Studios. John was the person who discovered and promoted the talents of Elton John. I had not yet met them.

Months went by and I heard that Rasmussen and Love Associates had been commissioned to do the plans for the Maitland's new home. Some time later I heard that construction would soon start. By this time I had designed and built many oceanfront homes and privately wondered why they never called me.

It was some time later that I received a call from Mrs. Maitland asking for an appointment. I set a date not knowing what they wanted me to do. On the day of our appointment they had just driven up from Los Angeles in a beautiful Porsche Carrera. They were both polished professionals who were a pleasure to meet and talk to. John was very quiet and Carmel did the talking.

They arrived with a set of drawings as big as a stove pipe. From the time I received Carmel's first call I was certain that they were looking for a builder. But it was soon evident that the purpose of their visit was something else. As she unrolled the drawings to the elevations and floor plans she asked, "I would like your opinion on these plans." I cautiously begged off saying, I can't be a critic because every architect has their own ideas. She quickly rephrased her question that she only wanted my feelings about the workability of the plan. She did complain about the long time they took to design her home.

I would not choose to be a critic of the architect but I did tell Mrs. Maitland that a serious oversight was that they did not consider the night view of the city. I added that at night the ocean goes black but there is still a beautiful view of Ventura. Carmel quickly rolled up the drawings and dropped them to the floor, adding, "You are absolutely right."

She added, "Bill, I want you to design us the most pizzazz house on the beach." She had written on a piece of paper the basics of what she wanted. There would be no discussion as to style or unusual details. I agreed to come up with some ideas that I would have in a couple of weeks. Our visit was possibly less than a half an hour.

106

Oceanfront home of Carmel and John Maitland

Their lot had a 90-foot frontage on the ocean. The new home would be a multi-split-level with an all cedar exterior with used brick. Facing the ocean was an imposing octagon structure that was the front entrance attached to a large exposed octagon fireplace shaft that had four fireboxes, one on each living level. One was in the front entry and one in the top of the octagon tower, the 'crows-nest' bar. Under the roof area was a refrigerated wine cellar. From the bar area a door opened onto a rooftop patio complete with BBQ kitchen.

The rest of the building tapered away from the entry tower with numerous windows to catch every view. In order to be more professional the sketches were redrawn on velum paper to be used as preliminary drawings, I called Mr. and Mrs. Maitland to tell them I had the preliminary drawings and we made an appointment.

I had not assumed that this project would be the work of a single set of drawings. And it is possible that a designer can so miss what the client wants that one must start a complete redraw.

When the Maitlands arrived at our home I spread out each drawing with an explanation of each sheet. When I finished, they both asked if I could build it. They asked me if I wanted a retainer, I replied no.

107

There would not be a single change in the drawings; there was never a discussion of what the structure would cost. With the completion of building details and engineering, the preliminary drawings would be used to build their new home.

The confidence that the Maitlands showed in my ability and the pleasure I received from working with them was a highlight in my life. I will always be thankful for their confidence in me.

It became a heady time in my life. The Maitlands' home had become a real statement for my ability. It was summer 1974 and Jeanne and I planned to make a trip to my parent's farm. Auntie Florine took care of our children and we made some budget-free plans for the trip. We first flew to Vancouver, B.C. and spent some relaxing days in a four star hotel and ate at the rooftop restaurant. From there we would take an Air Canada local jet and drop into every airport until we reached Winnipeg where we spent a night.

The next morning my brother Robert and his wife Avis met us and drove us to the farm. My brother was a very successful farmer and was beginning to dabble in politics. We were fiercely competitive and I am sorry to say it was not a vacation of 'brotherly love' but rather unabashed match of whom and what was best. Our biggest arguments took place in the demeaning of each others state. For me, North Dakota had not one redeeming merit. But we were still brothers and we were both very tough. After a week, he and his wife drove us back to Winnipeg and we said good-bye for the last time. My only regret is that I wished I would have hugged him and told him I loved him.

It was late October and I returned home midday to an empty house to check my calls. A note was draped on the phone that simply read, "Your brother Robert has been killed." In stunned silence I sat, not believing the note. Finally, I bravely called and learned his pickup had been struck with a grain truck; he died instantly.

My parents were proud people with children who had done well. They were people of little faith and the loss of their 'favorite son' was unbearable. The excessive display of grief and their attempts to blame someone else for the tragedy disturbed me greatly. It was the first time that I can honestly say, I was not proud of my parents. There were two funerals for Robert, as he was an important man. I did not go back to his funeral and was well chastised for my 'heathen-like' disregard for the pomp of a real Lutheran funeral.

Over the next months my grief for my brother was deep and without answers. The greatest of which was, "Where is my brother now?" The mere contemplation of the truth would make me cry easily.

I had to have answers and there were none, at least none I was ready to accept. I struggled through the winter months but I could not shake the loss of my brother. My once agile and trim build was starting to sag and weaken from the good life and I decided to find a gym with a well disciplined routine. I am sure it was a classic 'male burnout' resulting from too much stress in order to achieve something intended to be worth while. Whatever brought needed change to my life was beyond my understanding at the time.

The gym was located in the nearby community of Oxnard connected by only one good path from Ventura, the freeway. The path also put me in the shadow of two high-rises that boasted the best radio antennas in the area. One was a Christian station with a signal so loud I was forced to hear things I was not ready for, like the raving of 'Bible pounders' or the Gospel. I had two choices, turn off the radio or speed up, I chose the latter.

One day I caught a station that would capture my attention like none of the other religious ones. It was two Messianic Jews (Christian Jews) from a program originating in Chicago. The very first time I listened to them I was struck with their simple and straight forward presentation of the Bible as though it was an engineering manual or a serious volume on ancient history. What made their dialogue so believable was the tone of their voices, one not tempered with fire or emotion. Was it providence or simply luck, I don't know, but I was one of their new listeners. My morning schedule revolved around these two men.

It was a message I had never heard before. But one day I was running behind schedule and a program that followed was Oliver B. Green, an ancient rusty voiced evangelist from the south with one message, "We are all sinners!" When I reached the parking lot I shut off the engine and heard his voice pleading as though I were his son. I muttered to myself, go ahead and say what you have to say. I cradled my head on my arms resting on the steering wheel in my little Porsche and it was as though my life replayed in reverse. I was doing what few men ever do, retrace their footsteps and put their lives in proper perspective.

It was April 1975 and in June I would be 50. One of the things I had to reconcile was that I had waited 25 years for my M.S. to return and it never did. My dreams as an architect had been realized even without a credential. My reputation as a quality builder made it necessary to schedule work a year in advance. But even so, there was still the crisis of arrhythmia and heavy medication I had to live with. This time, unlike other successful men, I had to reckon with why I had been so favored.

The demand for my services showed no signs of letting up. However, my new found faith was taking me in as different a direction as there was Another to share my load. All the grief in the world was of no value on my brother's behalf. Change had to come to me and it did. The first big victory was kicking my 10-year Valium habit. The second was to come shortly.

It was early 1976 when I got a phone call from a very important man in Los Angeles. His name, Al Sakaroff. He said he and his wife had been in Ventura the past weekend and saw the Maitland home and asked if they could see me and discuss their new retirement home on the beach. A time was set.

After I met the Sakaroffs it was obvious that they were very accomplished people. I met them in our house on the sand dune and we got down to business very quickly. Mr. Sakaroff was a no-nonsense professional. Mrs. Sakaroff was far more reserved.

After our short time of greeting, Mr. Sakaroff said, "Bill, I know that you don't have an architect credential, but I want you to design our new home." He also added that he was the owner of the Los Angeles Commercial Sheet Metal Company. He also added that he works with some of the biggest architectural firms in Southern California and he could get plans drawn for free. My first thought was, what did he need me for?

Just as quickly, he added that they loved the Maitland building and they wanted that look. But of course it had to be different. Once again I had the job before I made the first sketches. Their basic requests were simple but with some special features. Mrs. Sakaroff was the Dean of Languages at Cal State Northridge and needed a large study. Mr. Sakaroff wanted his den sitting on the second level overlooking the entrance to the marina. He also wanted a large atrium entry because this type of structure was his company's specialty.

The structure also incorporated two octagons. One contained the spiral staircase and the octagon on the waterfront was Mrs. Sakaroff's study on the first level and Mr. Sakaroff's den above, complete with a fly-bridge crossing over the entry below. Four brick fireplaces gave the place a welcome look and six-foot-wide halls displayed their art work. An all cedar exterior with copper trim and used brick made the structure look at home by the sea. And once again the first design was built.

On Christmas 1977, the Sakaroffs held their open house. It was an evening affair and when we arrived it appeared everyone was there. Most of the guests were from the Los Angeles area. The place was well lit and the front doors were open to the atrium. As we approached the front door we could see that all the help was dressed in black and white. Drinks were served in crystal and served on silver platters. That night, dinner was traditional Beef Wellington with Yorkshire pudding.

We hardly stepped in the front door when Mr. and Mrs. Sakaroff greeted us. As Jeanne and Mrs. Sakaroff left, Mr. Sakaroff introduced me to a couple standing by the entry. The gentleman was quite tall and very distinguished looking. Mr. Sakaroff introduced me as his architect and builder and added that the gentleman was the President of Cal State Northridge. Mr. Sakaroff left to get me something to drink.

Oceanfront home for Mr. and Mrs. Sakaroff

Alone with the couple, the gentleman asked me how long I had known the Sakaroffs. I told him less than two years. His first response was that they have known the Sakaroffs, for 15 years and that this home is an honest projection of the Sakaroffs personalities. He added that their big home in Los Angeles did not reflect their tastes as well as this one. I thanked him for his compliment but added, "I gather you like what you see?" Of course the gentleman and his wife both were generous with their praises of the project. I quickly added, "What if I told you that I have no architect's degree and only a high school education?" The gentleman was shocked and his answer was that of disbelief. I knew I had his attention and I made sure I said what I had wanted to for at least a year.

Without hesitation I told him that my talent was a gift from the Lord and I cannot take credit for it. I made sure he understood that I have no elaborate design office and that the ideas flow naturally and that it is my clients who inspire me. The gentleman's wife said abruptly, "Bill, please wait here as I want to get someone who needs to hear what you just said." She was back in a minute with an important looking pair and introduced them. The man was the Dean of Psychiatry at USC. The story was repeated with coaching from the gentleman's wife.

That night I would have only one drink and no Beef Wellington. For the duration of the evening I spoke to an audience of giants and spoke the simple praises that my gift was from the hands of Another. It was late when my wife reminded me it was time to leave. When we left she asked me what I was talking about. She was excited at the things that had now become important to me.

Weeks later when I met Mr. Sakaroff he said, "Bill, I don't know what you told our guests at our open house but you sure made an impression." Today I cherish the words of King Solomon when he said in 'Proverbs' — "Show me a man who is skilled with his hands and I will show you a man who will stand before Kings." (The word 'kings' translates, 'men of power'.) That night Bill Vivatson stood before kings.

As the final curtain was about to fall on my career as an architect and builder in Ventura, I would owe hundreds of people a special thanks for their contribution to my career. I only called attention to the Maitlands and the Sakaroffs as it was so exemplary of what miracles can happen in one's life.

This chapter in no way depicts an artisan who embraces every skill associated with education and detailed training. But instead I was only a simple person with energy and enthusiasm who never learned to say "I can't." But there was, I believe, a greater message in what happened to me in Ventura that I would later learn. Sometimes I think my autobiography should be read backwards, I believe it would be easier to understand.

In late 1975 I volunteered to give blood one Sunday at a Red Cross center set up in the Ventura Community Presbyterian Church. During the routine screen an alarmed nurse told me my heart beat was too erratic to give blood. I assured her that this was normal for me and that I wanted to give blood. She kept a good eye on me and insisted I see a doctor. I didn't.

But quietly and with purpose I set about on two serious projects. One was to convince my wife to buy a larger piece of property near the beach but overlooking the beach park with a full view of the ocean. It was zoned for apartments and would be a good retirement investment. She agreed. The project was a large three-level structure that consisted of a cluster of octagons with a cedar shingle exterior with copper trim and used brick. It had several apartments and in June of 1976, once again, I would move my family.

The last dream house of the Vivatsons at Pierpoint Beach before moving to Hawaii

Simultaneously, I was looking at serious ocean going sailboats. There was one last childhood dream that had to be satisfied. That was, take my own sailboat on a journey to Hawaii and return. For the last few years I had read all I could about this ocean passage. I studied celestial navigation and had firsthand information about deep water cruising from my friends Bette and Dale Edwards who had been on long trips to the Caribbean.

On December 20, 1976 I had received my new sailboat. It was a Fisher 30' ketch built in Plymouth, England to my specifications. It was shipped to New York on top of a freighter and from there to California on a flat-bed truck.

I could never guess how this new adventure I had planned would have life-changes flow from it. All I knew was that those who had chosen me to be their architect and builder of choice were making this journey possible.

Jeanne, Laura, Claire and Bill Vitatson in May, 1977

CHAPTER TEN

Journey of *Still Waters*

It was June 1, 1977 and *Still Waters* was tied to the dock at the Ventura Yacht Club and we would depart for her first ocean crossing at 12:00 P.M.

On the dock were my wife and two daughters with our little dogs. Some of our friends were there to see my crewman Brendan Geary and myself off for a trip to Hawaii. My family would join me later.

Still Waters was a serious boat. An old European designed sailboat for cold weather sailing. In the days of pure sail, these small sailing craft were used to shuttle sailors from shore to ship in all kinds of bad weather. She had high freeboard and a weatherproof wheelhouse. Although it was built of fiberglass construction, it was built heavy with the North Sea tradition. With red bark sails, a forest green hull, white cabin and well embellished with teak, she had the look of tough and traditional class.

Still Waters was my second boat. The first was an Erickson 29 that was a nimble coastal boat that was recognized as a Marina Del Rey (California), 'Martini boat'. That meant on weekends you sat on your boat, with sailing friends, at dock sipping cocktails and talking about making a sailing journey.

My plans for the journey were long and cautious. To learn celestial navigation is the strange art of adding and subtracting abstract numbers collected from a sextant, perfect time from a short wave radio (Grenich time) mixed with numbers collected from two thick manuals. When worked properly, one can easily navigate the globe as if it were a road map, providing you can see the sky. There was also an endless list of safety gear that left absolutely no tolerance for forgetting the necessities.

Food and drink is what makes an open sea passage memorable. Offshore sailing, like few other sports or adventures, is burdened with constant stress, fear, anticipation and real tests. All of which consumes calories and enhances ones appetite. Even the long night watches of staring into a dark and empty night encourage the need of constant snacking.

A long trip at sea makes mealtime the highlight of the day. The life expectancy of fresh food at sea on a small boat is very short and soon everything you eat will come from a can or box. For this reason it takes some real planning to come up with an interesting variety.

One of the priorities of survival at sea is water. Our supply was carried in two large reinforced plastic tanks with several gallons stowed in the emergency inflatable survival raft. Hundreds of cans of sodas were stowed aboard. Alcohol is a dangerous traveling companion because emergencies need a clear mind. We will eat well and often.

To make the transit easier, she was fitted with a Volvo Diesel with 1000 mile-range of diesel. Both a wind vane and electric autopilot would permit her to move hands off. A couple weeks before leaving Brendan and I took a four-day trip offshore to nowhere to see if everything worked. We were ready.

The fear of the ocean is justified, but it can be managed. Too often it is fear that keeps most sailors at home. To remove any reason for excuses, one must name a date of departure and leave as stated. My declared departure was 12:00 P.M. June 1, 1977. The date was set five months before. It was after the delivery of *Still Waters* in late December 1976 when I told my family that I would leave for Hawaii June first. But also on that December day, my proclamation carried another weightier consequence that would be the beginning of my retirement. My coveted career as an architect and builder ended with my adventure on *Still Waters.*

With the nonchalance of an over-confident sailor I said good-bye to friends and family, climbed aboard with Brendan, started the engine and cast off. Decades later, and much more cautious, I often think that I was reckless. But today I know there was Another who had scheduled this dream of a poor boy long ago. I was 51.

It was a sunny windless day and with empty, flapping sails we motored into a windless sea.

There had been so much preparation that it was hard to believe we were bound for Hawaii. It would be about a three week journey. Brendan was only seventeen (he would turn eighteen on the journey) and came from a sailing family of Irish heritage. He was an enthusiastic and capable companion. His father worked for me and his mother was an R.N. She had put together an elaborate first aid box for us, even potent antibiotics in case we had appendicitis. The boat was outfitted with an emergency locator beacon and every safety device conceivable.

With no wind, we motored across the channel and passed between Anacapa and Santa Cruz islands. It was only about 25 miles out to sea. There were several islands that lay to the south of us that I wanted to be sure to stay well clear of. The wind was light so we continued west on the engine. About dark the wind picked up and we reduced the amount of sail that was up. As the wind freshened, we cut the engine and engaged the wind vane.

In June the channel winds tend to diminish, but not tonight. Before long a howling gale pressed us to the south. We were fearful of getting too close to the islands to the west of Long Beach so we opted for a very rough ride with the wind hard on our starboard beam. *Still Waters* was a full keel vessel with extended rudder so she was in her element. It was as if she grabbed the sea in defiance that propelled us into the waves. Not so for Brendan, he became very seasick. As the wind howled and water smashed against us like driving rain, *Still Waters* seemed to gallop over the now rolling seas. The enclosed cockpit was a worthy investment. Sailors tend to suffer in open cockpits because it is very traditional.

117

We were not in the shipping channels but for safety sake I carried two radar reflectors and a strong strobe light on top of the mast. In the middle of the night I felt it safe to drop off to a southwesterly direction. As of now *Still Waters* was traveling the fastest and in the roughest waters of her young career. I was very satisfied with her performance and Brendan was very sick. He would not even respond to my questions of concern. The cockpit had a large comfortable seat, stacked with huge comfortable pillows with a safety seatbelt. As the night went on I became so tired I would catch myself dozing off — not a safe practice so close to land. This is most likely why real sailors sit out in wet, cold, open cockpits.

As the sky began to lighten the waves still slammed against us. I went down to check on Brendan, but there was no way he would be joining me in the wheelhouse for breakfast. As the sky lightened a thorough search of the horizon showed me that we were alone. Not a trace of ship or land. For some reason I am not troubled with sea sickness. It could also be my Viking roots. Emboldened with tough sea legs and sea stomach, I went down below for something to eat. It was too rough for anything hot so I grabbed anything available and returned quickly to my seat and strapped myself in to relax.

It was soon full light with a hazy sunlit sky that turned the sea a light powder blue when it dragged breaking water from wave to wave. The color was something I had never seen before. In the full light, I started to survey the rigging from inside. She had sailed herself all night. My only hands on was an occasional remote adjustment of the wind vane. As my sleepy gaze went to the wind vane, I was shocked to see one of the pulley clevis pins on the rudder connection had come loose. I tried to get Brendan up to help me but it was no use, he was very sick. I was just lucky that he didn't tell me he wanted to go home. I got my safety harness on and safety cable hooked up. I knew better than try to touch the barely holding clevis. I simply got a heavy piece of wire and tied it together. If it had come loose the boat would have turned sideways to the wind and seas and we would have had some trouble. Sailing is very dangerous in gale force winds because the strength of mere men is no match. When things go wrong in a gale your only hope is to hold on and not be swept away.

This storm showed no signs of quitting. The white foam still reached from wave to wave. I knew the offshore islands were no longer a threat and I decided to make life easier for us and let the boat fall more to the south. That meant the gale winds would be pushing us nearly south. Not necessarily the right direction for Hawaii, but still a gusty ride for *Still Waters.* My new boat far exceeded my expectations. Weary and tired, I felt an excitement in my new adventure. Brendan had been asleep for hours but I was very thankful he was here with me. Thanks Brendan.

The hours slipped by into afternoon. Although I was stretched out on the bench with a couple big pillows, I could see in every direction. I was beginning to wonder if this was what sailing to Hawaii was going to be. By late in the afternoon it was time to force Brendan to wake up and eat something. With a stove equipped with pot hold-downs, I prepared some hot food. After we ate there was only one place Brendan wanted to be, back in bed. My sympathy for him was best exhibited if I let him sleep for as long as he wanted. As the second evening approached I checked the rigging carefully from the wheelhouse. I went below and pulled up some floor boards to check for any leaks. What I should have done was to run the Volvo for awhile, but the battery still showed full charge and I was satisfied. All was well for the night. I made myself comfortable in the wheelhouse with the big pillows and a thick blanket and rested my weary body. I felt I had been awake for a week. I knew by now we were well out of the shipping channels and stress most likely was making me careless. I turned on all the exterior lights and the strobe. I turned off all the cabin lights. I switched on the stereo, shoved in Rick Nelson's tape, "Garden Party" and strapped myself in for the night. *Still Waters* crashed confidently into the waves in a southwesterly (Hawaii) direction. I could not remember when I was so tired.

The final days before departure were fitful nights thinking about what I might have forgotten. I can only wonder how much I had slept that night. But I do remember waking at early dawn and *Still Waters* was charging long rolling seas at a fast pace. As the day brightened the world looked different. The water was a different color than that of Ventura. It was a cobalt blue. The long rolling waves had short white caps breaking at the crest as if dancing. It was exciting, and finally Brendan answered to a 'get up' call. There was even a change in weather as a full sun climbed high in the sky. We were still moving at a good pace and it was too rough to find out where we were with a sun shot. We were on a direction of Hawaii and we agreed to check tomorrow.

I decided to start the engine to charge the battery. As it started there was a loud BANG and it started. An inspection revealed that my brand new Volvo had broken a valve pushrod. It meant that we could only idle the engine to charge the battery but had no power for motoring. That meant we would sail all the way to Hawaii with a full tank of diesel. I was a mechanic long enough to know repairs would be easy when we reached Hilo, but for now we were a sailing vessel. The performance of *Still Waters* was so remarkable I was content to revel in her lively pace. She was a real sailboat and I wasn't going to let the failure of the Volvo spoil my trip.

Up to now Brendan and I had been beaten to near 'Zombie' status. Our weary bodies were adjusting to the sea and ready for food, drink and conversation. Stress had overcome us, but now we were recovering.

On the morning of the fourth day, a clear sunny sky and a nice wind pressing the sails from the starboard beam, Brendan and I felt we had fared very well. Long, strong swells came from the same direction as the wind causing the boat to rock in slow motion as she headed southwest. Brendan was well, but would rather slip back into bed than enjoy seeing the sea slip under our keel. We were headed in a safe direction so I decided to wait another day to establish where we were.

We were so lost the next morning we gave up and opted for a 12:00 A.M. noon shot which is known as a latitude sun shot. We had to have perfect time at high noon and take the shot. This would give us a perfect line as to how far north we were from the equator. Later in the day we took a sun shot that put us on that circle that crossed the latitude shot. We were able to put our finger right on our location on the globe.

We were over 500 miles west of Mexico and over 400 miles south of Ventura. We were shocked to find that little *Still Waters* had traveled at hull speed (maximum speed) for nearly four days and we were well on our way to Hawaii. Our first reading of the trailing log, a distance measuring device, showed we had traveled over 600 miles. *Still Waters* was a going machine.

The sailboat hustled along, shoving strong wavelets off the bow. She had a stiff ride that permitted us to fix our first real hot meal. It was Brendan's choice. After four days it was good to have someone to talk to. As night approached, we made plans to have Brendan do the watch until 12:00 A.M. He had already slept all day. As darkness fell, all the running lights were turned on and I got him set up on the comfortable captain's bench and I went to my bunk, first time in over four days.

It was not long before I got up to check on Brandon. He was sound asleep. I woke him and said he would have to sit straight up in order to stay awake. Obediently he lifted his head off the big pillows and sat up. I woke again to check on Brendan and he was sound asleep with his head against the cold cabin window. Keeping him awake turned out to be a hopeless cause. From then on I would stay in the wheelhouse all night, and during the day I tried to get some sleep below with Brendan topside.

By day six, life aboard was a routine of mostly taking care of ourselves and faithful *Still Waters* did everything else. A wind vane is a device that keeps a sailboat on a relative course in relation to the wind direction. The vane frame is bolted to the stern. A vertical moveable wing will want to point directly into the wind. This wing is connected mechanically to a small rudder that in turn is connected to the tiller. A line connected to pulleys extends to the cockpit door so you never have to leave the wheelhouse to change course. The one on *Still Waters* was the best made (Larwick) and from the time we caught the winds past Santa Cruz Island until we started the engine to motor into Hilo, Hawaii harbor she was on her own. The wind took her all the way with the wind vane doing the steering.

By now a full mainsail was up and a large and powerful Genoa (front) sail was up. The rear mizzen sail has little driving power and mostly used to balance the boat and take the pressure off the rudder. This new sail plan would not be lowered until we reached Hawaii.

The trip to Hawaii could be called a sleigh ride if you pick the right season, as we did. We were moving south every day. On the globe Hawaii lays 1000 miles south of Ventura in the tropical belt. Every day the weather was getting warmer and the color of the ocean turned to a pristine blue. The wheelhouse door was always open and the skylight was pushed back. Each day the wind is moving from the starboard beam (port side of boat) to the stern. Onboard there is a tremendous aura of self-sufficiency and well-being. A stereo with cassette player was our companion as the mainland radio signals faded away. Often the energetic roll of *Still Waters* seemed to match the beat of the music. The wheelhouse has become our haven from the constant fatigue of

Still Waters *being driven by the power of trade winds*

the wind. It protects us from a rough swell that would slap the hull with waves that could get us wet. The large shelf below the windshield was well supplied with books, magazines and tablets. *Still Waters* was a faithful servant that would not stop until we reached Hilo. For the entire passage we were never without wind.

This journey could not be measured by days but rather events as we traveled from a temperate climate to the heavenly tropics. About midway to Hilo, when the wind was directly behind us, we were in the 'tropical trade wind belt'.

The word 'trade winds' have a magical quality not only in word but in its inherent physical phenomena as a part of our tropical weather system. The trade winds only occur within the tropical zone of 23 degree north and south. (This is the maximum north to south travel of the sun.) It is the only wind system that has its primary direction from east to west. It is said that the fast spin of the earth at the equator drags the air mass with it. The dependable force of the trades within the tropic zone is determined by where the sun strikes the tropic belt. In our summer, it will be north of the equator. In our winter, it is south of the equator. And right about now we are traveling right under the path of the sun. That means we are in the full strength of the trades.

When the day came that the magical power would come directly behind *Still Waters* it was an experience that had its roots in my childhood. The word, trade winds, was part of the jargon of the Pacific story tellers of the 1920s. And for me, decades later, for almost three months I would revel in its magic.

Instantly a sailor knows when it arrives. The first indication is its caressing warmth. It is a natural comfort zone for the human body and swim trunks are all the clothing you will need, night or day. For the rest of the journey to Hilo, little *Still Waters* rolled with gusto.

The day the trades came behind us, we set the full main and Genoa sails, one stretched out on each side. An aluminum pole was used to stretch the genny to catch the full wind. Both sails would be tied in position. This a point of sail called 'wing and wing.' The trades blow night and day in the same direction but usually ease up at night. At extreme it could reach perhaps 40 M.P.H. But for our trip it must have been 15 to 20. The full keel of *Still Waters* let her handle full 'wing and wing' like a champ. With the wind directly behind, the wind vane mechanism was dancing as if it were facing a balancing act. This direction of sailing makes different vessels do strange things. It is not a desirable point of sail. For *Still Water* the motion felt like a duck waddle as she rolled from side to side. As the winds increased, the driving power made her bow slam the waves in defiance.

At first Brendan and I were very apprehensive about our 'wing and wing' point of sail and sort of expected the pressure on the sails, rigging, mast and wind vane would cause something to fail. But after a couple days our confidence was in my little old-fashioned English vessel.

As the days slipped by, the euphoria of this portion of the journey was beyond description. The wind vane was the single most important accessory that made a small sailboat enjoyable.

Out here the sea was a void. The only fish we ever saw were two flying fish that ended up on deck. One day when the trades were only gentle blow, Brendan asked if we could tie him in a heavy line and pull him along. We started the engine for safety as he put on a life jacket and mask to check the water. In the balmy water he was having fun. He paid little attention to my calls for him to get on board. Until, in a panic, he let out a holler to chase away an albatross with a huge wing span. The large bird mistook Brendan for flotsam.

Our living routine settled into an idyllic moment of living the adventure. We were becoming so relaxed that we would have lost track of time were it not for the records we used for navigation. Each day came and went without a problem. The day arrived when we would pass under the sun, this meant we were south of the sun. In the mainland we are always north of the sun. That meant when we would make our sextant calculations all the math would be in reverse. We had a large near blank map of our path across the Pacific. It only had the coast line of part of California, Mexico and the Hawaiian Islands. The blank space was lined with latitudes and longitudes. Our daily sun shots tracked our journey as if we were professionals. It was a wonderful trip. Brendan was well over his motion sickness and was always up and around. He was great company.

When we finished our afternoon sun shots, we fixed dinner. The ritual was intended to kill time. Every compartment like those under seats and bunks were packed with canned food and drinks. There was enough to last for four months. Brendan would dig around until he found things he liked and we made a dinner out of his choices. A very small electric refrigerator permitted us to have cold drinks or cold canned food. Our fresh produce like carrots and potatoes were ruined by the tropical weather. Dinner was a big time of our day.

There is nothing like cold water and chilly air to convince a sailor that he really doesn't need a bath. But once we reached tropic waters, a bucket of sea water over the head on a hot day was a real treat. Liquid kitchen soap worked well in salt water. It was a necessary ritual because we would never dare jump over for a dip. Life was simple as *Still Waters* kept us on the move and on course. We were far from any shipping routes. We had the sea to ourselves so at night we turned on all the exterior lights and went to bed. Sleepyhead went down below and I slept in the wheelhouse with the big pillows. At night the sea is so black all that is visible are the stars or another vessel.

There were two incidents that happened, both at night time, that caused us some moments of concern. The first incident occurred well after dark as the boat was making good time under partially cloudy skies. We were getting ready for bed and Brendan was dragging up the large wheelhouse pillow for the night. As he came up from below, facing the stern, he shouted, "Ship astern!" Sure enough, a small but strong light was well astern and would confuse us as to its direction. We started the powerless engine in order to make severe course changes. Any attempt to change our course did little to improve feeling of safety. The strobe was blinking, and we even turned on the marine radio to channel 16, the international emergency channel. Our calls, "Do you see us?" went unanswered. As the broken clouds separated we discovered it was a shaft of moonlight on the horizon that had looked like a light from a ship.

Another incident followed after a few nights that really panicked us, and we would never know what it was. It occurred about midnight when the boat was moving under light winds. There was a strange noise like the running of the automatic bilge pump. The noise would reoccur at well-spaced intervals. The sound simulated the vibration of an electric motor changing speeds as its sharp sounds were transmitted through the hull. During these were the times, we were calling Russia the 'evil empire'. One of Russia's many methods of intimidation was to cruise their ships and subs between the Hawaiian Island. This sound continued for a considerable length of time until it became a steady sound and faded away. Could it have been a sub traveling on the surface that saw the powerful strobe and took a look? We would never know.

Brendan taking a last sun-shot before arriving in Hawaii

It was in the last week of our trip to Hilo and the trades picked up strength and long following seas were dragged along. For both *Still Waters* and me it was a new and threatening adventure. The waves came as predicted and as the afternoon developed the motion of the boat made Brendan and I very nervous. The Larwick wind vane had been dancing for days to keep *Still Waters'* stern face directly into the wind. Today her new challenge was to negotiate the sharp cresting of an overtaking wave and safely ride down the back face. The great danger is when the waves are too steep and too close together and the bow might dig in resulting in a life threatening motion called 'pitch poling'. Our little boat had a very high bow that was very buoyant and the long keel produced enough drag on the down slope to keep us safe. If the boat is too light it is necessary to drag a sea anchor to slow the vessel. Our sea anchor was one of many safety items that were never used on this journey.

For hours we studied the miraculous gymnastics of *Still Waters* and the wind vane and decided we could trust her. She was not an Ericson 29. The following seas of the trades are a body of water that lifts and falls from the pressure of the trades. For several days we galloped along with these monsters. There is a strange feeling that the boat is sailing both uphill and downhill.

The last couple of days before landfall, we noticed the trade swells were losing their power and size. It must have been the influence of the land and mountains. Riding the trades in balmy weather had been an adventure.

One afternoon, after our last shot, the math said we would see Hilo in the morning. The last night the seas were sloppy and confused. The closeness of land changes the wave pattern. The wind kept us moving and I did not sleep that night. Brendan went to his bunk and I was comfortable in the wheelhouse listening to a Hilo radio station. As a fitful dawn broke and some scattered rain clouds tried to make way for the sun, I spotted a couple fishing boats. I called Brendan to get up and help me spot Hilo. When he came up to the wheelhouse, strong reaches of sunlight pierced the cloudy skies and all of a sudden white blocks appeared on the horizon. A good look revealed the blocks were the high-rise hotels. We were right on course!

The view from sea in unfamiliar waters is both confusing and fearsome. From Hilo north for 50 miles there is a shear rock face where strong waves pound constantly. We were fortunate sailors. It would be an hour before we would start to search for the opening in the break-water. Brendan was as nervous as a cat. Soon there was a new experience for us as the soft fragrant aroma of a tropical land swept over *Still Waters*. It was a fragrance of earth and foliage. We had spent three weeks in a sterile seascape. At a time like this, the feelings are most likely simple excitement. Brendan and I were cautious seamen and we never considered our arrival a victory, we were simply happy to get on land. Our destination was before us.

Before we entered the breakwater, I started my well-rested Volvo. As we motored toward the sailboat wharf Brendan spotted the Koehuts' sailboat from Ventura. It was not the boat that excited him but it was his high school buddy who was aboard. The year before the Koehuts family had sailed to Tahiti and was now returning to Ventura. We hardly tied up to the dock and Brendan was gone.

It was early afternoon when I got things put away, and to register with the harbor master. I didn't have to go far to locate Brendan, he and his pal had a whole year to catch up on. I pulled him away long enough to find a phone and tell my wife we arrived safely. And after that we went to look for a steak dinner. Late afternoon I visited the Koehuts as they shared their adventure for the past year. It was a good night's sleep on a bed that stayed in one place. The first night on land Brendan and his buddy sat on the dock and talked sea stories until early morning.

Jeanne arrived in Hilo in a few days, bringing a new Volvo push rod and a new strobe light for atop the mast. The first one wore out. When she arrived, the plan was to sail to Kona but the Alenuihaha channel was so rough we decided to drive instead. We left Brendan in charge of the boat. Our few days in beautiful Kona were enough to prompt us to invest in a piece of vacation property. Most of the ma-neuvering would be mine; I was becoming well aware that my natural comfort level was that of the tropics. But I was unaware it would soon become our home.

Back in Hilo, the Volvo had a new part and we prepared to leave for Maui. The winds in the Alenuihaha Channel had abated, but the best time to make this rough ride would be late night. Our trip to Lahaina was about 110 miles and could take 20 hours. After we left Hilo, we traversed the east coast, well offshore, for about 50 miles.

About midnight we turned west into a black channel about 12 miles wide. A trailing marine odometer would give us an exact measure of mileage when to make the critical turn. Further into the channel we should see a lighted buoy that would confirm a safe passage. Now it was Jeanne's turn to be sick.

The channels that separate the Hawaiian Islands can be treacherous places. The tall mountains flanking the channels tend to compress the trade winds that increase their velocity and ability to drive big waves before them. A couple years before, a large (40-foot) sailboat disappeared in the Alenuihaha never to be seen again. The dark night and rough passage would end in a glorious sunrise with Lahaina in the distance and the sails would go slack when the island blanked the trades.

As we traversed the western shore of Maui, my crew decided to come up and act alive. Brendan had stayed with me through the night in the dangerous channel and I had been up all night. That was the negative of being a boat owner. Worry was my constant companion when *Still Waters* was at sea.

The sunny shoreline was a long line of green trees and long stretches of beaches. To our west was an ancient blown out crater and to the north was Lanai. It was a beautiful sight to see the mountains rising above these warm blue waters. There was no wind, so we motored and lowered the sails.

Lahaina was a very interesting and low profile town of another day — long row of interesting old buildings, housing, shops, and restaurants lined the shore. It was a very inviting village. Soon we were motoring through a number of anchored sailboats into a compact harbor with a carnival like atmosphere.

Still Waters was the first known Fisher ketch to sail from the mainland to Hawaii. When we made our way to a crowded guest dock, the harbor master was there to meet us. Several signs warned of permitted dock use. Only a few minutes was allowed for servicing. A smiling harbor master approached us and asked what kind of vessel she was. When I told him he was all the more curious and asked if he could come aboard for a better look. He was quickly invited aboard. His response was, "Of all the sailboats I have ever seen, this is the one I want."

I knew that marina docking was impossible, so I asked him where

Still Waters *at Lahaina Harbor*

the best spot to anchor was. To our surprise he pointed to a slip occupied with a large powerboat. He said that it would be leaving for Honolulu for a week and we could move in it tomorrow in appreciation of giving him a tour of beautiful *Still Waters*. We anchored out in the bay for the night and in the morning when the slip cleared, we moved into the in town marina. It was a whole week right in the center of Lahaina, free.

Our itinerary was a casual one that gave us over three weeks before we were to meet our daughters in Honolulu. After our week of luxury in a slip, we headed for Black Manele Bay on Lanai, a primitive little harbor with small wooden docks surrounded with shade trees and bath facilities. Jeanne had brought with her plenty of reading material to keep herself occupied. She had taken over the job as cook, and Brendan and I were out exploring. It was an idyllic moment in my life that I most likely shrugged off as routine.

One day we hitched a ride on a truck to Lanai City. It was a small plantation town high on the top of the island in a pine forest that whistled in the wind. We checked every store and found a small cafe for something to eat. Lanai was a pineapple plantation island and, as we walked to the edge of the village for a ride back to the boat, I spotted a warehouse.

It was a place that the pineapple was trimmed, tagged and boxed for shipping. I asked a gentleman if I could buy some. With a surprised look he grabbed an empty box, filled it up and gave it to me.

As we reached the road to the bay, the first person who came along gave us a ride back to the boat with our supply of pineapple. Manele Bay was a busy place. Close to the harbor was a beautiful white sand beach and picnic grounds. Every day several boats brought tourists to the island for a day at the beach and lunch. As they walked past *Still Waters* they would give smiling glances of admiration for the jaunty little ship. Everywhere she went she drew attention. In a couple days we left for Maui with a new supply of pineapple someone else gave us.

One morning we headed back to the Maui Kaanapali coast. A place with long stretches of beautiful beaches. We anchored close to a beach that was well protected by the island of Lanai. One evening the three of us got dressed up for a change, and rowed our Avon inflatable into shore to have dinner at a hotel. As we approached the beach, I was rowing the dingy to get us close to the beach. Brendan was to jump onto the beach with the line. He was to hold the line tight until Jeanne and I got out. Jeanne and Brendan stepped on the beach neat and dry but for whatever reasons, my untrustworthy companions let the dingy slip into deeper water. In shear frustration I jumped out to do the job myself. But when I jumped it was in a six-foot hole of water. My revenge was to make them walk around the hotel grounds until I drip-dried for dinner.

On another sunny morning we started our six-hour trip to Kaunakakai, Molokai. We motored through calm waters shadowed by the tall mountains of Maui and Molokai. There was only one short passage between the islands where the trades filled our sails. We traversed the rugged and vacant shore line with coral reefs stretching well out to sea. At one time we panicked when we saw coral beds so shallow that we would collide with them. We cut the engine and slowly retraced our path back to deeper water. We were careless sailors.

As we reached the harbor at the north end of the island, we entered a windswept harbor crowded with pineapple barges. It was not a comfortable or attractive place and we decided to stay only a couple days. We motored deep into the harbor to attempt to escape the strong wind but we had to be satisfied to let the boat swing on one anchor. The constant day and night gusts of wind that swept across the bay made for restless

Still Waters *anchored off the Kaanapali Coast, Maui*

nights as *Still Waters*. Kaunakakai village was a fifteen minute walk up a steep hill. An adequate grocery store supplied our needs and some treats. A very small hotel on a secluded bay was a place for a good meal but there was little else here and we were anxious to move on.

By the second day we were checking the weather to prepare to cross the Molokai Channel. I guessed the channel between Molokai and Oahu to be at least 25 miles, but a safe curving route to the west would place Honolulu a good 60 miles distant. The Molokai Channel can be a treacherous stretch of water when the trades blow at full force. The high velocity of the wind forced between the two land masses can produce gale force winds for days. When we wanted to head for Honolulu, the gale force conditions kept us in barren Kaunakakai for another day. We were running low on pineapple and across the harbor I could see pineapple palette boxes stacked by the hundreds. Brendan and I decided to row across the bay and ask for a couple. An over-generous dock hand picked out at least a dozen choice pineapples and we were stocked for another week. Our boat smelled heavily of the fresh, pungent fruit.

Our lazy pace would have to change as Laura and Claire would be arriving in Honolulu in a week. A night crossing was safer because the winds tended to diminish. We were into the fourth day in Kaunakahai harbor and we were checking the weather forecast every few hours. Always the same, the channel was under the siege of gale warnings. *Still Waters* was a hardy boat that could go anywhere under small craft warnings. However, gales are dangerous conditions for sailboats. The strength of mere men is not enough to manage even small sails in these blows. Into the fifth day there was more of the same. My anxiety to get going kept me on board playing cards and checking the weather every hour. A long day of disappointment passed and that evening Jeanne prepared spaghetti for dinner. After dinner I reached up and turned on the marine radio. A familiar sounding voice came on, "Molokai Channel has been reduced to small craft warnings." I shouted, "Let's go!" Had I known what peril we were about to face, I never would have left!

By now the sun was setting and the Pacific night falls fast. The first thing I did was was start my trusty diesel as Jeanne put away her five day kitchen set up. Brendan went topside and deflated the Avon dingy and secured it tight on deck. The lazy sailing for the past three weeks in the

The author and crewmate, Brendan, off Molokai

lee of Maui and Molokai would come to an end fast. Everything inside and out was secured and checked. The storm jib (small front sail) was hooked and the main was reefed in short. I connected the electric auto pilot for the crossing because if things get rough the boat under power will hold a better course. As we hauled the anchor and chain aboard we had to start motoring or be driven by the strong wind onto the banks of the harbor. I was concerned, but glad to leave this windswept place. All the lights were on, including the strobe. It was maybe illegal, but I wanted to be seen. I let Brendan and his sharp eyes pilot us out into the night-black harbor and place us on a loop course for Honolulu.

My plan was to set a course well away from the huge waves of the channel. There was a normal but rough chop to the seas as we cleared the harbor and were out in open seas. The engine speed was increased to calm the rolling motion as we passed the lee of Molokai. Within a half-hour we were feeling the power of long rolling seas driven by the trades. My conservative curving route was no match for the broadside strikes of these rollers. I let the boat fall off to the port (left) and take the brunt of the waves more on the buoyant stern. But a new problem was I would be heading into the island of Lanai. There was no choice except return to a sail direction with the wind and waves on the starboard stern. It was going to be a rough ride and there would be no going back or even think we could find the entrance of Molokai harbor. I kept a course that would miss Lanai, but it was going to be a long way to Honolulu. The long powerful waves lifted *Still Waters* like a cork. White caps would strike the starboard beam and seawater would shoot into the air and swamp the deck. The seas were glowing with algae.

As of now I was alone. Both Jeanne and Brendan were deathly sick. There was no pleading or threat big enough to get Brendan up to help me. The skies were clear and the moonless channel had numerous shipping vessels with lights that would have to be avoided. The most dangerous were tugs pulling freight and cargo barges on long cables. Each barge had its own set of lights. My strobe was making strange reflections on the surrounding waves.

We were committed to the channel no matter what. The night was warm and the wheelhouse door was locked open. The wheelhouse sunroof and cabin ports were closed to keep seawater out and there was no fresh air for my crew. This was a year when the phenomena of seaborne algae will blanket a huge area of the sea. When the water is disturbed it glows an eerie frosty green. And tonight the seas were streaked with this strange calamity and made the waves look all the more foreboding.

I lost track of time, and my concern would be to hold a course clear of Lanai. By now I should have been able to see the lights of Honolulu, but the combination of the fast building seas and the algae-lit water was all that was visible. We were now on a course that took us out to sea rather than to Honolulu.

The wheelhouse was totally black except for the ghost red light in the big compass. My faithful Volvo was pushing us at hull speed. (6 knots) and I stayed clear of all lights. The seas were so confused it was impossible to determine the height of the waves. The velocity of the wind was intense, but the sails area was so small it was not dangerous. But what was happening was we were getting away from the narrow part of the channel. The waves started turning into long rollers that would lift *Still Waters* into the air stern first and then slide under her in a fast slap of breaking white caps. I was very concerned that things were going to get worse. I never had been in a sailboat with such huge seas. There was no escape. Whatever stuff *Still Waters* was made of, she traversed these mountainous waves as though it was what she was intended to do. The powerful gale wind screamed through the vibrating rigging as if to taunt us. It was a frightening night.

Soon the glow of Honolulu lit up the horizon and the wild, roller coaster ride became so euphoric I was driven to shout and holler as each swell made *Still Waters* dance as if animated on the crests of these monstrous following seas. I tried hard, but unsuccessfully, to get Jeanne and Brendan to take just one look at what they were missing. I dashed down below and soaked a towel in water and tried to wash their faces, but they were out.

Sometime in the middle of this perilous night I crested one of these monstrous rollers and spotted a very bright red light dead ahead and slightly to starboard. It was soon evident the red light oscillated from red to very bright red. It was the U.S. Coast Guard in position for a rescue. It is nearly impossible to correctly judge distance during the hours of darkness. The direction of the light was my desired course. I opted for the shorter and passed above the emergency light. As I changed course, *Still Waters* took a little more beating but before long I knew we were well clear.

As the red light slipped past us, we moved in the direction of Honolulu. Before long the wind began losing its power and the rolling seas were losing their height as well. It wasn't long before the Volvo was making more noise than the night-long gale.

We were approaching the place where the island of Oahu became a protective block in the path of the powerful trades and high seas. It was still very dark and the coastal lights that stretched for miles were very welcome.

The Volvo Diesel had propelled us along all night with practically no sails to help. I had not touched the wheel since we cleared Kaunakakai harbor. The only course change was made on the electric autopilot. *Still Waters*, at only 30 feet long, was a formidable challenge to the fury of the Molokai Channel.

As the waters flattened and the winds died, I sat alone and quiet. I can't remember what I was thinking, but I know it would have all the emotions present after a near miss accident. The thought entered my mind that I should have never left the safety of Kaunakakai Harbor but as my anxieties faded, I started thinking of more imminent problems. Such as, we were arriving in Honolulu just as the Pacific Trans Pac sailboats were arriving, where we would berth?

During the early morning hours of darkness the trades were gone and long gentle swells lifted and lowered *Still Waters* rhythmically as she rolled from side to side under power. I was fighting exhaustion and sleep. Just in time, a streak of light mercifully heralded a calm and clear new day. We were still well offshore from Honolulu. It would be daylight before we turned in the direction of the small boat harbor. A quick look down below told me no one was interested in sharing my long anticipated arrival to Honolulu by sailboat. The only signs they were alive were their high body temperatures. The watertight cabin smelled like misery. I went below and unlatched the forward hatch and opened all the ports. I wet some towels and tried to engage Jeanne and Brendan in some communication, but they remained silent and motionless.

Back on top, *Still Waters* was rumbling along headed for the Rainbow Hilton tower, a very tall structure with the ceramic tile mosaic of a rainbow. It sits directly behind the yacht harbor. The sun was well above the mountains and it was a great new day.

As the channel buoys came into view, I made one last attempt to threaten Brendan to report for duty. It was hopeless. I throttled back the diesel, disengaged the autopilot, and took the wheel. I had rehearsed my arrival to Honolulu many times from looking at the harbor charts. As I entered Haleiwa Yacht Harbor channel, I looked for the fuel dock and quickly spotted it. It was not even 7:00 A.M. The diesel was at low idle as I approached the fuel dock. A short engine reverse and *Still Waters* came to a full stop and we drifted to the dock. The calm made it easy for me to step to the deck and tie up. The fuel dock was not open. I cut the engine and let Jeanne and Brendan recover. On the dock, I slowly moved about on tired legs and paid little attention to my surroundings. I went back aboard and found something to drink and sat in silence.

Trying to kill time, I walked up the dock to the fuel pumps. I passed a very large sailboat. On deck was a middle-aged man in swim trunks busy at something topside. We recognized each other with a weak good morning. I did not notice anything was wrong with the boat. Then I noticed huge stainless steel turn buckles hanging over the side on huge chain plate with short pieces of cable attached. In a flash I was wide awake and saw the mast was missing. I asked the gentleman, "What happened?" His reply, "We were dismasted last night." My reply was to ask if it was in the Molokai Channel. His response was, "Yes we (he and his wife) were coming from San Diego." I asked, "Was that you being rescued by the Coast Guard?" I was answered with another, "Yes." He looked back at little *Still Waters* and said, almost sarcastically, "You weren't out there in that were you?" I answered, "Yes we were." Our conversation abruptly ended as he busied himself with his chores. His boat was a large, heavy and expensive 46-foot Cal a recognized world cruiser. He later told me that the heavy gusting wind and heavy seas broke his mast and the entire rig fell in the water so they could not motor. He called for the Coast Guard and they came alongside and cut all the rigging and sails loose.

After I fueled up I decided that either I wake up Jeanne and Brendan or call a doctor. I had partial success in coaxing them topside to see the beautiful spot we were in. And it was beautiful. From the fuel dock one could see from the airport to Diamond Head. Directly in front were the famous Waikiki Beach and an impressive row of large hotels. Below the clouds on the horizon was a green mountainside. I was getting anxious to reach the yacht club.

The fuel dock attendant told me that the yacht club office did not open until 9:00 A.M. I had a whole hour to contemplate our wild

Still Waters *at the Honolulu Yacht Club*

journey of last night. My wasted crew were so worn out they did not want to hear about it and retreated below. I had a solo experience.

While I was waiting for the yacht club office to open, I was anxiously anticipating my reward. There was a decade's long tradition of the Honolulu Yacht Club giving anyone who sailed their boat from the mainland a free, two-week stay at their club. This generous offer drew many a vessel to these shores.

At 9:00 A.M. I called the yacht club manager and told him we had just arrived at the fuel dock. He gave me directions as to where and how to approach the club. He would be watching for us and wave us in. This time I got Brendan topside and fired up the diesel.

We approached the yacht club as instructed. A huge, two-story wooden structure sat on a green cocoa nut tree studded island. The attractive club house was surrounded with roofed balconies and was a welcoming sight. Brendan recognized two men waving us in the right direction. There were no docks in particular for guest boats. They pointed their bows to a wooden walkway surrounding the small island and the boats would be rafted together as many as three deep, all pointing toward the shore. A series of padded planks would permit you to reach the island by means of crossing the decks of your neighbor's

139

boat. It was a cozy relationship for the next two weeks. One of our hosts stayed after we were properly tied up to tell me where to register and where the basic facilities were. His last words were, "Where did you arrive from?" When I answered that we came from Kaunakakai last night he said nothing and just stared at little *Still Waters*.

There are moments in life when the fulfillment of a dream stands before you with such power you are speechless, like the birth of your first child. Every human emotion is traumatized and your only expression left is tears. And here I was, forty years later, standing on the deck of my own sailboat in front of the Honolulu Yacht Club. And my wife sound asleep below. My dream had come true.

I went onto the yacht club island to register and have a look and walked around the club. The first level was a sailors dream — spacious bathrooms with hot showers and a large laundry room. There were ice and soft drink machines and several large picnic tables. Upstairs reflected the best of Hawaii. A huge open pavilion-like structure with nearly a full 360 degree view, a large bar and dining facility. What a great place to spend two weeks!

When I was in the upper lounge area, a very loud announcement came over the P.A. system. The message was announcing the arrival of another Trans-Pac yacht. I think this prestigious race takes place every four years. The yacht club members would dock their boats elsewhere and the yacht club would host the race boats as well as the race festivities. It made for restless sleeping for the next couple days as new contestants received their P.A. welcome.

It was about lunch time and I went back on board and forced my crew to get up. We went to the club lounge, but I don't remember if they ate anything. I forced Jeanne to take a walk to the Ala Moana shopping center. It was about a half-mile walk and when we reached the upper level she spotted a large bench. She would go no farther. With her purse as a pillow, she went fast asleep. I had to stay close by so her purse wouldn't be snatched or keep her from being arrested for vagrancy. When she awoke she felt better and we made our way back to the yacht harbor.

As I was guarding my weary, uncomplaining wife, I was totally exhausted and functioning on some sort of inner strength. I had been awake since about 6:00 A.M. of the day before. I had my 51st birthday on my way to Hilo and everything had gone well. Our spectacular crossing of last night had not fully sunk in to my tired mind. There was no doubt it was a perilous crossing in such a small boat and our victory was one we lived to talk about. *Still Waters* would forever have a legacy as the smallest sailing vessel that made this dangerous passage.

When Jeanne and I returned, Brendan had recovered and was out inspecting the real sailboats, the world class racers. He came back all excited about what he saw. I went with him to take a look at these powerful, fast vessels of world-class competition. Many of these boats had shared the gale force winds with us in the Molokai Channel last night. As we reached the docks Brendan pointed to the broken masts that had snapped at the top spreaders, bent at right angles and the mainsails still tied securely to the broken masts. There were possibly a dozen damaged vessels.

To see the damage done to these high-tech sailboats was a very sobering experience. And only a couple hundred feet away was little *Still Waters* in flawless condition ready for another crossing.

As Brendan returned to our boat, we were just in time to see the yacht club helping tie up the big Cal 46 with the mast torn away. Brendan gasped to see the damage to such a trustworthy vessel. Brendan was a purist when it came to sailboats and believed the Cal 46 was the only true cruiser. When I told him that we passed near the Cal 46 when she was being rescued by the Coast Guard, he could not believe it. Little *Still Waters* was classed as a motor sailor, but she could sail. Now Brendan would have to give her some respect. In the following days, people came down to the deck where *Still Waters* was rafted with the other boats to admire her. I knew their conversation was about the little boat that was in the gale the night the Trans-Pac boats were dismasted.

That evening we had an early buffet dinner at the yacht club and called it a day. For years we would have much to talk about.

These were casual days at the yacht club with Jeanne looking for shady spots to sit and read. Brendan was a person who explored everything and made acquaintances easily. The only damage from last night's journey was a badly chafed Jib halyard (rope) that had to be replaced. As I made a thorough inspection of *Still Waters,* I had to consider how easily I had adjusted to the journey that was about in mid-point. It was almost two months since I had left Ventura. I was very proud of my selection of sailboat, but there was another change of direction stirring in Bill Vivatson. I was never a person who had to hold on to what I had achieved if I saw something more rewarding ahead. But this time in my life I felt a need for change but I did not know what. I was not one to leave a project half-finished and the change that was coming would bring with it a new set of challenges.

At the end of our two week stay at the yacht club, our daughters flew into Honolulu for a vacation. They went directly to their hotel and then walked over to see us. It seemed so long since I had seen them — they looked so grown up. Claire was 17 and Laura was 19, about the same age as Brendan. They stayed at their hotel because five aboard *Still Waters* would be a little tight. We spent time together until it was time to leave the yacht club.

My childhood dream of sailing my own boat to Honolulu was now history. I chose to spend every day of my allotted two weeks at the historic Honolulu Yacht Club. How wonderful it was. On the day we left, the girls moved on board and instantly the boat got smaller. I checked out and thanked our host and prepared to leave. It would be a big job to untangle us from the scores of rafted, cruising sailboats. But before long I started the diesel and we motored out of Alawai Yacht harbor. The mighty Cal 46 was still waiting for her new mast.

We headed up the coast to the west past Pearl Harbor. Our first stop would be at Pokai Bay on the Waianai coast. It was a beautiful spot with a long, white, sandy, tree-lined beach. It was the place the locals lived. We spent about four days here and ate either Chinese food or pizza almost every day. The three 'kids' rowed back and forth to the beach on the dingy. Brendan met a young soldier who played guitar and invited him to the boat one night for dinner. After dinner we sat out on deck while the soldier played for us. The last day at Pokai Bay, Brendan went to Honolulu on the bus to buy a spare part for the Volvo. He made a full day of it and didn't return until after dark. We had the dingy tied up to *Still Waters* and kept watching for him. Late at night he swam out to *Still Waters* in his underwear. He was all upset because we couldn't hear him calling. I rowed him to shore to get his clothing and the engine part. After we got back to the boat he told us about his day and all was forgiven. Brendan was a good guy to be around.

The last stop before heading to California would be Kauai. It was another overnight passage in order to make a trip with less wind and waves. The channels are very unpredictable and caution would make it safer. We headed out from Pokai in the afternoon in the direction of Kauai. We motored for several hours in the balmy lee of the island of Oahu. Everyone was up in the wheelhouse taking turns steering. It was the time when I told them there was considerable traffic at night in this channel and I would need some help. They all promised their eager offers of assistance.

Before sundown, and before we were in the channel, we had our dinner. My young sailors were all fun, hungry and excited. We had to get the cabin ready for those who would sleep in shifts. Because of sea sickness the two bow bunks were unusable underway. Also the front bunks were now piled high with sail bags and luggage. In the main cabin there were three bunks for my four passengers. Three would sleep when one would take a turn helping me look for trouble ahead.

Before long it was dark and *Still Waters* was starting to go through the unsettling motions of climbing up one side of the rolling waves and sliding down the other. Jeanne had learned that once the boat got under way she went to bed. As the seas kept building soon Claire went down to get in bed with 'Mama'. It was not too long before we would be broadsided by heavy seas and near gale force winds. Once again the sails had already been shortened, the Volvo running and the electric autopilot engaged. Tonight I had to hold the course for Nawiliwili Harbor or miss the island. There was no option to a very rough ride.

Laura and Brendan were real competitors and both were determined to help me in the wheelhouse. *Still Waters* was hustling along but heeling heavily. Their bench was on the high side of the cabin and they had to brace themselves as the waves struck the side of the boat. Soon the mighty waves struck us one resounding 'bang' after another. The waves, shooting in the air, flooded the front deck. Soon Brendan went down and climbed in the small berth under the wheelhouse floor next to the Volvo. And Laura was getting quieter by the minute.

Laura retreated to the security and comfort of the cabin but soon returned to inform me there was no bed for her. I told her to grab all the blankets she could from her shipmates and make a bed on the floor. Once again I was alone. In no way did this passage compare with the Molokai Channel, but it was a real ride. It was something my daughters still remember.

It was daylight before I heard from any of my passengers. We were still a distance from the harbor and they were all coming alive and hungry. When I looked below, the place was a mess of clothing and bedding scattered everywhere.

Once again I made another night passage with *Still Waters* doing all the hard work. Everything was lashed down tight. The short sails were up and the Volvo was rumbling the sweet beat of a marine diesel and the electric autopilot was in charge of keeping a tight course through the night. But as usual the captain never gets a break.

The sun was up and the near vertical walls of the island were a beautiful rich green. It was a wonderful welcome. Oahu tends to have a brown look from the dry hillsides. In the early morning, we motored into a very green and beautiful harbor with steep mountains covered with palms and other trees. My crew was all up and well rested and willing advisors as to where we should anchor. We picked a spot close to the pier and to keep the boat in position we put out two anchors. It was an easy row to shore. After my young crew ate a whole box of cereal they were ready for a day of excitement.

Nawiliwili Harbor was an exciting spot for a cruising sailboat and crew. It was a place for larger boats and freight barges with a well protected harbor that was home to the fishermen and a large hotel with generous and cheap buffets that we frequented often. Our three wards were continually hungry and having fun. I think Brendan made their vacation.

Near our end of the pier was a very large hippie-style camp ground complete with toilets and showers. The very large shower area was about the size of a six car garage with no roof on it. At one end a large sign read 'men' and on the other it said 'women'. The good intentions of the park service to provide a secure divider had been foiled by some naturalist that completely removed it.

The first order of business for my female crew members was to take their towels and soap for a shower. When they discovered the co-ed facilities there was heard a whoop and a holler and quickly guards were placed at the two entries. Except for the daring naturalists, most showers were taken after dark. For some reckless reason my young crew thought it was great fun.

A few days after our arrival we met a kindly elderly Hawaiian who was a self-appointed dock captain for the sailboat cruisers and fishermen. He stopped by to introduce himself and said we were invited to the Saturday night potluck. The simple instructions were that everybody brings something to share. Bring your own drinks, plate and fork.

In a few days it was Saturday night. By the time we arrived with our offerings the evening had started. A large, half-barrel BBQ was fired up with our dock captain as cook. Several large fish wrapped in foil were cooking. A huge picnic table was overflowing with food. The guest list included fishermen, many local people, campers, aging hippies, pot smokers and us. In the few days since our arrival *Still Waters* was a 'smashing' hit. She was so beautiful floating at the edge of a tropical jungle. Her shiny green hull and jaunty white cabin all topped with gold anodized masts and teak trim would catch anyone's eye. Many boaters and people asked if they could come aboard and look at her.

After our first party, we rented a car so we could haul groceries and do some exploring. The three kids started their morning by consuming a whole box of dry cereal, and were ready for whatever came along. One place the youngsters were excited about was a steep, sandy beach on the east-facing shore, the windy side. As the waves broke on

Jeanne, daughters Laura and Claire in Kauai

Jeanne, the chef, relaxing after dinner

Our favorite beach on Kauai

the shore the water shot up the steep beach. They found great excitement catching a wave and being propelled up the sandy beach. Their fascination with these short waves kept them busy for hours. There were trips to Hanalei Bay, Port Arthur and Waimea Canyon and the daily trips to the grocery store. I don't think we fully understood that we were on a high adventure of a lifetime. We just enjoyed each day.

By nature I am a cautious person. Solutions to my problems are usually found before trouble finds me. Our journey would have us crossing all the seagoing traffic from California to all of Asia. This traffic would last the entire length of our return trip. Here sea safety depends on our seeing them before they hit us. There was one dilemma that I was faced with that, as yet, had no solution. That was that the moton of the sea made Brendan a hopeless sleepyhead. His happy and easy temperament made him impervious to threats or coercion to stay awake.

Our friendly dock captain was a masterful host and invited us to our second dock party. This Saturday night we were having fish as well as BBQ turkey. The second party was even more fun because we had come to know more people. Anchoring in Nawiliwili had been a wonderful experience. To wake up every morning to the chatter of a thousand birds in the warm tropics has few comparisons. And add to that there will be at least a week of more of the same. The three kids were fun to watch. They were spoiled and didn't I know it. But now those days were running short and I needed a third crewman to have that extra pair of eyes. I spread the word around to the dock people about my needs and even told our dock captain. That night a young man named Frank approached me for a ride back to California. He was from Michigan and worked in the automobile industry as a model sculptor. He also reeked from the pungent odor of marijuana. I detailed the responsibilities of boat safety and that there would be no smoking of anything on board.

I took Frank over to meet Jeanne and the rest of the family. No one was impressed except Brendan. To him, Frank would be a friend for the long trip back. The rest of the night would be spent having fun and eating. Life by the dock had become a real social event like being at the Honolulu Yacht Club.

During our last week I was beginning to dread the long journey back home. September was the last safe month to traverse this passage. Our last days together as a family were those of resolve. I would, with the help of my crew and *Still Waters,* complete my childhood dream. My family would leave Kauai by plane and be home in hours; I would leave Kauai and not be home for a month.

The next few days were busy stocking the boat with a month's supply of food and drink. The hundreds of pounds loaded aboard nearly three months before were nearly gone. The water tanks were flushed and filled with fresh. The diesel tank filled. As a precaution several five-gallon cans were filled with diesel fuel and tied down on deck in case the 'Pacific High' was too persistent. A condition where there could be no wind for a full week or more.

Our last Saturday night dock party was a joyful time, but also bittersweet. The hospitality was generous and added greatly as the 'grand finale' of an adventurous summer. As I made the rounds to say goodbye, I was aware that Frank was flying high on pot. There was no purpose in worrying, since he was my only offer for a free ride to California.

Only a few days later, on a sunny morning near the end of August, *Still Waters* was tied up to the dock. Our rental car was nearby and being loaded with all the things my family brought with them. Frank arrived early in full hippie regalia — worn out denim shorts in shreds, long, flowing hair and bandana.

The good-byes were short as my family left for the airport to turn in the car and catch their plane. The summer party was over. Frank placed his things aboard and the Volvo rattled to life. We untied the lines and motored into the open and unforgiving sea. Since this day of long ago I often wondered where was my sense of fear or concern. To this day I often ask myself what kind of fire drove my life that made impossible dreams so ordinary. Perhaps I will never know.

Well clear of land, we attempted to set a point of sail to the northeast. The tides were hitting us from the wrong direction, so we had to motor for several hours. As we reached a favorable wind direction, we pulled up full sails and *Still Waters* was bucking heavy seas. By dark, Kauai was a distant blur and we were heading home — very long way. I glanced at my watch and estimated that my family had arrived in Los Angeles. I felt so alone. I guess dreams do have a price.

Frank was a real bonus. Only once did he attempt a late night hit of pot. When I caught him, he was apologetic and full of remorse. It never happened again. Frank was a natural-born sailor who had only one other sailing experience. He liked the night watches as he listened to music on the headsets. Brendan still was hooked on his full nights of sleep. And Brendan had a real pal in Frank.

An interesting relationship developed between them. Frank was a real rebel and Brendan was a 'want to be'. Our relationship was strong because he knew I tolerated no nonsense. Brendan was a brilliant young man struggling with too many frustrations of youth.

The next morning we saw only a world of water. We were pounding as we attempted to keep the boat on a northeasterly course. The driving wind was on our starboard, forward of the beam. This continued for days and there were times that our point of sail would place us farther to the west of where we wanted to be. In fact, for several days we were getting closer to Japan than California.

The sailboats returning to the mainland always have a bad time because of the undesirable trade wind direction. For us, we would have to travel north by northeast until we were on the same latitude of San Francisco. For a full week the wind was on our starboard. At the far northerly point, we hoped we would curve to the southeast with the prevailing wind on the port side.

By now *Still Waters* was beating as close to the direction of the wind as possible. The pounding of the seas on her bow was merciless.

149

Still Waters *trapped in the doldrums of the Pacific High*

So much water was splashing on deck, we stayed in the wheelhouse. Frank was becoming the caretaker of *Still Waters* during the hours of darkness. In the daytime he took long naps. He asked if he could set up his own space in the forward berth. This was a place that no one can find comfort or rest. It is the place that pounds in rough seas and a sure place to get seasick. But Frank loved his haven and privacy. It was his suite until we reached Ventura, a long way off.

Our greatest pleasure was either eating or sleeping. Cooking was a challenge because *Still Waters* heeled heavily from the force of the wind. About the seventh day we took some serious sun shots to decide where we were. The check of our trailing odometer read about 850 miles from Kaui. *Still Waters* for all her other good attributes could not head into the wind very well. We would have to be patient.

On the eighth day, early in the dark of morning, our little boat was rolling crazily in the short swells and the sails and rigging were slapping and banging for lack of wind. It was not a good situation for a vessel meant to sail.

After daylight it was obvious we had run into the fabled 'Pacific high'. As the sun rose into the sky with higher temperatures, our world looked like a wet desert. We pulled down the sails and tied them down. We fired up the well-used Volvo and motored at a moderate idle speed. This moved us at only four miles-an-hour but it conserved fuel. We carried over 1000 mile-range of fuel. We kept our northeast direction until we reached the latitude of San Francisco. There was no other option.

Frank made our long journey home a very civilized adventure. By now he understood the doldrums could go on for days and also it would not end with a gale but rather a slow shift of the winds to the north. *Still Waters* had a deep front deck where the tall gunnels made a secure place to sit and relax. Frank asked if he could bring pillows and mats up for comfort. Of course, it was a great idea.

The midday sight indicated we had to travel north for at least three days before we reached latitude where the winds could take us to southern California. *Still Waters* was under control of the very precise electric autopilot. The Volvo was equipped with oil pressure and engine temperature alarms so we could relax up on the front deck where our wet desert let us enjoy swim trunk weather. It was time to recover from the constant pounding of the rough windswept seas. Frank served us lunch on the front deck. The big supply of electricity from the Volvo permitted lavish use of the electric refrigerator and lights. Cold drink and food are a luxury at sea. A wonderful dinner was prepared by Frank, with Brendan's enthusiastic help, in a galley that was, finally, level with the earth. We ate up on the front deck and enjoyed a desert sunset on the flat seas. The two were like little boys digging in food storage lockers looking for the good stuff. They dug through the canned food and packages for new treats.

One day they found a tin of Chinese fortune cookies. I was busy with something else, but I could hear them reading the silly fortunes aloud. After some time Frank called, "Bill, how about a fortune cookie?" As he passed the tin, he was right, there was just one left. I took the last one and opened it up to see the piece of paper with the fortune. I handed it to Brendan to read, it said, "You will have a sweet home in Hawaii." Ridiculous.

There were two large stereo radio/cassette players aboard with headsets. Both boys spent long hours listening to tapes. I had brought along a set of tapes by J. Vernon McGee, a renowned Biblical scholar. The tapes were a complete study and conservative commentary on the Bible. By now I had listened for hours to Mr. McGee on my watches. One day, I am sure out of boredom, Frank asked how I could listen to those tapes so much. I told him I listen because it is a story of all mankind for the ages, the past, present and future.

It was not long before Frank listened for hours to Mr. McGee's tapes and asked serious questions about what he had heard. I was seeing a different side of Frank. He was a man of deep comprehension that belied his rebel appearance. Brendan was an interesting person. His rebellion was a screen to cover his many frustrations. Then one day Brendan declared, "I think I would like to listen to the same tapes as Frank." It was interesting to hear them share what they had learned.

The 'Pacific High' was a high pressure zone over this vast area this time of year. This high pressure area was so vast and invasive that it would not permit the flow of other weather patterns that permitted any winds from any direction. It was a place that had a foreboding mystique which made you feel insecure. As the very hot sun passed over us, it caused a surface glare and haze that made sunglasses mandatory. After close scrutiny, you could see that it was a floating dump. The entire area of perhaps hundreds of square miles must have a circular motion that caused anything that floated to be here. There were pieces of rope, wood, produce crates, plastic bottles of every size and shape. Of course there was lost fishing tackle of every description. There were sometimes vast stretches of fish netting kept afloat by huge plastic balls. The prized Japanese glass floats caused Brendan to demand the boat be stopped so he could retrieve them. Most were small, about the size of baseballs.

One day Brendan spotted one of these floats and wanted the boat to stop so he could pick it up. I said, "Brendan you have enough." With that reply he simply jumped overboard to retrieve it. That was our impetuous Brendan. But what made the whole scene look like a dump were the endless bits of Styrofoam everywhere. I know this is hard to believe, but if you concentrated on the water around you there would be some physical reminder that man had been here. One morning Brendan was leaning over the bow of the boat looking for something interesting and called back for Frank and me to come and see something. When we went forward, he showed us several small striped fish following the breaking water in front of the bow. They were pilot fish. For a week to come, this became one of Brendan's daily rituals, watching his little friends follow us across the sea.

It was here that I found the reason why the Albatross cruise the vast seas. They find food on the flotsam. If you picked up a piece of board or anything that floated it was inhabited with large gooseneck barnacles well-attached.

One day Brendan shouted, "Sailboat!" As it approached Brendan, a race boat expert, recognized it as the *Merlin*. It was on a fast motoring mode that overtook us quickly. They pulled close and asked if everything was alright. We said it was and questioned if we were on the right course for California. Their positive reply also said it would be a few more days until we hit wind. Very soon they were out of sight and our little boat purred on alone. Interestingly about 15 years later I met a man in Kona who was onboard *Merlin* that day. It was an interesting coincidence.

The 'Pacific High' was a place we saw too many freighters to count, all large and moving fast in both directions. In daytime there was no problem because their path was obvious and we could maneuver if they felt too close. But at night when we spotted one, all hands were on deck to be sure we did not get in their way. We always tried to reach them on the marine channel 16 to check our position or just to talk to someone. No one answered. It was another sunny day and Frank and I were down below sleeping. There was a panic shout from Brendan, "Freighter!" As I dashed up the companion way, facing the stern, I was horrified to see a huge black and rusty hull and nothing else. As I grabbed for the marine radio microphone I realized he was nearly dead in the water. As we all calmed down, we reached the captain on the radio. He said they were concerned because they could see no one aboard. Of course not, when Brendan was on watch he always looked for a corner to slouch down and take a nap. This watch he was curled up on the wheelhouse bench in sound sleep. At this time in Brendan's' life nothing was important or serious.

Who knows how long this Philippine freighter was ghosting us. With Brendan on watch it could have been for an hour. And from the lofty position atop the freighter they could never have seen him in the wheelhouse. I am certain they had visions of this lovely little boat being a derelict prize. As we motored along slowly, we carried on a conversation with the huge freighter not far behind. They asked if we needed water or diesel. We could have used both just to top off our supply but in my many years of 'dream' reading about sailing I learned never to let strangers on your boat at sea. I begged off on the offer but asked them for our position. He gave it to us and I asked him his destination. He was traveling to Long Beach, California. I asked him if he could call my wife and tell her where he last saw us and I gave him an approximate date we would arrive in Ventura. Later I found out he did call Jeanne, and as luck would have it, my estimated time of arrival was exact to the day.

After the freighter left, we pulled up our marine odometer and found out we had traveled 1900 miles since we left Kauai. We made the afternoon sun shot and it agreed with the freighter's navigator. We had been underway for almost three weeks. Ventura had to be less than a week away. We were all getting homesick and we were about out of diesel. Brendan and Frank had a new hobby, eating. I knew we had plenty of food but it was the variety that was starting to suffer.

We cautiously motored through the night with the Volvo at full idle to conserve fuel and tomorrow we would have to wait for wind. The next day, with very light wind, we slopped back and forth in light swells and the Volvo was silent. This meant there was wind somewhere. The same day we had a new crisis, no fresh water. The natural carelessness of youth is a burden that all of us seniors and more enlightened must carry. There is never enough fresh water in a boat for either a bath or washing our hair. Brendan and Frank decided that long hair made them look like real sailors and they had been swiping fresh water for rinsing their long locks. No scolding was necessary because they were both embarrassed and ashamed of the gravity of our situation. Fortunately there were enough sodas and canned drinks to finish the trip. By afternoon there was wind.

A journey such as this can either be one of contention and a waste of time or it can be full of pleasant surprises and special things to remember. The journey of *Still Waters* was rich with the latter.

It would only be a matter of hours from the time the first air filled the sails of *Still Waters* until she was being propelled at hull speed with the north wind hard on her port. Once again she bit into the seas with her long lead keel to brace the stiff wind and drive us to California. It was the next day when the large genny was removed and the smaller jib hauled up. The weather built to a nasty, near gale wind that never stopped for days. She slammed and banged against the sharp waves under a cloudy sky. It got colder and soon the wheelhouse door stayed closed. Only a hand reached out now and then to adjust the Larwick wind vane to a better point of sail. And Frank still called the bow his domain. Mr. McGee had become his traveling companion. The night watches became a twosome as we approached California. I think we were more aware of the many freight boats and wanted to get home alive.

One morning, after we had slammed into choppy seas all night, Brendan got up and placed his feet on cold and wet floor boards. With a tone of surprise in his voice he called, "Bill, there is water on the floor boards!" Sure enough, and there was a lot of it. Two bilge pumps ground away for an hour or so to pump it overboard. It never returned and we never knew where it came from. It was getting more difficult to get our sun shots. The seas were very rough and the skies were constantly overcast. We were only a couple of days from California's infamous Point Conception and, if there was any chance to see the sun, we caught a shot any time of the day. Soon our course was solid as though we felt as confident as if we were reading a highway map.

On the last afternoon we got excellent sun shots that told us we would reach the farthest north island of the Channel Island chain. It was a barren desert-like tall island without any buoy lights and it was a dangerous place to approach at night. Slightly to the north and about seven miles from the northern tip of the dark island was the light of Point Conception. We carefully read the trailing log to double check our distance to land fall. The last reading recorded distance traveled from Kauai was almost 3500 miles. We had traveled an incredible distance to make this passage. I had the added safety of both Frank and Brendan in the wheelhouse for the whole night. No captain could have had better. I made hot chocolate often and dug around for something for them to eat to encourage their concern for our safety. They lowered the windshield to look directly into the darkness. There was high excitement. Tomorrow it would be 26 days at sea.

Long after midnight the excited voices of the watchmen said, "Here it is the coded flashing beacon of Point Conception!" We had safely passed the dangerous dark island without ever seeing it. As we headed in the direction of Point Conception it was still very dark. It was impossible to see how far we were from the light, so we slacked off on sails to slow our move toward shore.

As the first break of day occurred, they spotted land safely in the distance and we were in the coastal channel. We could now head south to Ventura, about 60 miles away. We were still trying to keep sailing to save diesel and we were too anxious to get home to stop in Santa Barbara for fuel. By the time we reached Santa Barbara, we double checked our fuel tank and found there was plenty to reach Ventura.... I called Jeanne on the marine radio and told her we would arrive about 4:00 P.M. We stowed all the equipment and sails and my able crew packed their possessions. We were all excited to see Ventura in sight. Our joy could be best described as euphoric. It is strange how men would submit themselves to the stress of such a demanding journey, but, in the end, we were unbelievably happy. We had a successful journey.

Eventually the breakwater of Ventura Harbor was in sight. We rounded the southerly point and entered the channel. It wasn't until we passed the large land banks that protected the marina that we heard air horns blast to welcome us home. On the dock were many friends to greet us. Even Bette and Dale who had encouraged me to buy that boat before I was too old. We were home safely. There was not a single cold or mishap for nearly four months. It was a wonderful summer. A summer of a lifetime.

Still Waters *returning to Ventura Harbor*

There are profound moments in life for everyone. Times when incidents, planned or otherwise, are so profound one is lost for a proper response or statement. For me it was the birth of my children. Today, it was the culmination of a forty-year dream that by all odds and expectation would be just that, a dream. To take a small vessel on a 6,000 mile journey requires endless hours of preparation and considerable expense. The unforgivable demands of the sea force one to trust to memory the skills of celestrial navigation and seamanship. And there was the constant fear that I would forget that one very important thing, whatever that might be. I managed the stress of planning the journey to the day that we left, but I was not prepared for the stress of returning home.

As we made the last turn into the marina, the blasts of air horns continued. My emotions were running so high I feared I might cry. It had been a safe trip. My family had lived a high adventure. I had lived a dream. My cup had overflowed. As I slowly pulled alongside the dock, willing hands tied up *Still Waters*. My first reaction was to reach for my little dog Mitzi to mask my breaking emotions. There were so many people there. It was good to see my family. It would be minutes before I could even speak.

Homecoming at the dock with my little dog, Mitzi

I was home. In a few months *Still Waters* would belong to someone else, and Ventura would no longer be home.

Afternote:

The night that *Still Waters* traversed the Molokai Channel in gale force winds that would later be recorded as a storm that would only occur every 50 years.

Khoa I Dang Refugee Camp in Thailand

CHAPTER ELEVEN
Retirement, Something New

We arrived in Kona March 8, 1978. Only twenty months earlier we had moved into our new retirement home on San Pedro Street in Ventura. We were both a little young for retirement. We left behind our two young daughters, Claire 18 and Laura 20. Also left behind were Auntie Florine and two very dependant poodles. They all continued to live in our new apartment building. Jeanne's car remained in the garage.

My wife carried a heavy burden trying to cope with my decision to move to Hawaii. When we left, I was certain that Jeanne had commissioned her friends to pray for a short stay. Whatever she had packed for the move were things she could have easily thrown in the trash before she moved back to California. Our portion of the complex was left empty, but it looked as though we were only on vacation.

Jeanne & Bill retired in Kona, Hawaii

Before our departure from Ventura, my entire energy was used to make our move a reality. My trip to our attorney would transfer the responsibility of completion of active projects to others and push for the sale of our properties.

As I write this, over 25 years later, it is still almost impossible for me to understand how easy it was for me to walk away from my career. There had to be something or someone that would provide me with such peace about my decision. I walked away from a career that would take some people decades to develop, but I simply quit after seven years.

My decision to quit had nothing to do with another plan I had in place for my life. I left with an empty plate and no agenda. My vision could see no further than the shores of Hawaii.

For those who knew me best, there was a serious concern for my sanity. Those who were willing to give me a pass would say, "Bill, what are you going to do with yourself?"

For me, our new life in Kona was one of smelling the roses and the joy of the moment. For my wife, it was a time of silent mourning in our new condo across the street from the beach. The worst thing about a change of location move is that you will have to be content with strangers instead of family or friends. Fortunately for us, we had met a couple from Canada who lived in Kona, Peter and Donna Jordan. They were an enthusiastic couple who were excited about their volunteer service at a local Christian mission. We were invited to join them in attending their fellowship and found ourselves comfortable with their mission of service. Both my wife and I are conservative people who are not easily swayed to do things we chose not to. Our friendship gave us a chance to meet new people, like us, who had also decided there was something else waiting for them.

The responsibilities we left behind made it necessary for us to return to California occasionally and this eased the pain of the move. We also had an added blessing when many our friends and family came to visit us in Kona. We soon found we were not alone.

The timing of our move was excellent because Kona had become a new destination for mainland retirees. Also there was a timely building boom that gave us confidence that we had not moved to a desert island.

Condominiums at best are a temporary place that can never take the place of a home. We were here only a couple of months when I was riding around on my bicycle looking for an ideal place to build a house. At that time there were considerable opportunities for the purchase of vacant land. It was a great place to invest, but I wasn't interested in that. However, I had my mind on just one place. We chose the oceanfront boulevard of Alii Drive and near the White Sands beach area. It was close to town and convenient. One thing I knew about retirement was that one should never choose isolation.

One day I spotted a beautiful lot only a block from the condo and across the street from the ocean. I told Jeanne about it and suggested that we find out if it could be for sale. A trip to our realtor, Billie, disclosed that it belonged to a local Japanese family. This choice was a long-shot because these are not people who are prone to sell their possessions. A day later Billie called and said they would sell it and the price was $35,000. For us it was a bargain and we purchased it immediately.

We promptly placed our condo on the market that we had purchased less than a year ago for $83,000. The Kona boom and demand had now pushed the price to $135,000 and we listed it with Billie. A few days later I changed my mind about the price and went back to Billie. I suggested the new asking price should be $148,000 and a reluctant Billie agreed. It sold in just a few days for full price. Both Jeanne and I felt that the good fortune of a beautiful lot at the right price and the timely sale of our condo would serve a blessed confirmation that possibly Kona was home.

We were in a well-developed neighborhood of friendly people. We designed a two story home that had a nice ocean view. I tried to do the right 'Kona things' like having enough windows. The exterior was made from my favorite material, cedar. It was a big mistake as the carpenter bees loved it. We had to have the whole house sprayed with poison.

It was the first time that I totally enjoyed building our own home. I had nothing else to do. I took a leisurely ride into the village in the morning for coffee that soon made possible the meeting of many new friends. When I felt like it, I started pounding nails. There was no threat of cold winter rains, no budget problems and no move in date to worry about. This was what retirement was all about.

It was summer 1979 and our new home was finished and we moved in. In a few weeks the last plants and trees were in the ground. Everything was finished. Right now I was starting to think, what next? I had never considered how I was going to manage my time. There had just been one thing on my mind, quit.

My love affair with the sea was still alive, so I ordered a small trailerable sailboat for exploring local waters. Here in Kona the waters are warm and pristine and there are endless coves and small, sandy beaches. All were devoid of development and population. There were three strategically located boat ramps, one right in the village. Kona in no way resembled the dirty cold waters and overpopulation of California. It was not too long until I knew what I had and I wasn't going to give it up or go back. The first two months I had the little boat I discovered places so beautiful that I revisit them dozens of times in the future. I felt like Huckleberry Finn.

But, once again, I found my life was in the hands of others, my doctors. My old friend, arrhythmia, had returned with a vengeance. I had cut off Valium for over five years and this time I found little comfort from new medications. I had little fear of my problem, but the condition would be so annoying that I knew I had to be serious about some answers.

A new prescription was added to medication and that was, no coffee, chocolate or stimulants. Added to this was a two-mile jog every morning. My early morning jog was along beautiful Alii Drive to Kahaluu beach and back. I filled in the rest of my days taking it easy or sailing in my new pocket cruiser. Life was simple and I wanted to keep it that way. I enjoyed the casual life of hanging out in some of the outdoor coffee shops in the village and meeting new friends.

My jogging program continued, and so did my problem. One morning when I reached my halfway point at Kahaluu Beach, I sat down and cupped my sweaty head in my hands. I never was a person who permitted despair to invade my life but this morning I was close. I loved to be in charge of my life without limitations, but now I was trapped.

As I sat there the news of the day must have passed my mind. At this time there were endless newscasts about the 'Killing Fields' of Cambodia. To say that I had any particular sensitivity about the situation of Asian people would be a lie. After all it was the Japanese people that prompted WWII that cost the loss of tens of thousands of Americans lives, and they also disrupted my plans for my young life. I remembered the Bataan death march that cost the lives of thousands of Americans at the hands of the treacherous Japanese.

However, what happened that morning on the beach reached far beyond delusion or emotion. Wherever the message came from, it would change the rest of my life forever. In the flash of a minute, and like the scrolling of a computer screen, were my orders. — Go to the Cambodian Refugee Camps on the Thailand border — leave now — take a green toolbox and basic tools. Perhaps it sounds like I am speaking with the naiveté of a fool, but it all came to be. It was late September 1979.

I ran back home and told my wife about my encounter on the beach. Her matter-of-fact answer was, "But first I want you to go and see your doctor." I was very surprised that she so easily accepted my message as though it were in a printed document. However, I should have known that Jeanne was a wise person who had grown accustomed to watching her husband make choices and decisions that someone else must have been orchestrating.

Later that morning I went to see my doctor about my latest plans. His quick and frustrated response was, "Your condition is so precarious that even a small accident could put you into shock." I was a little embarrassed by his bluntness and simply said thank you and left for my truck.

I sat in my truck for a moment thinking how much I hated this moment when I could not make my own decisions. How well I remember placing both my hands on the top of the wheel and placing my head on them. I know I wanted to ask for help or a clear decision but nothing came. When I made my decision to go it was as though my body got the message at the same time. The truck door popped open and I went to the nurse's office and told her to order my shot package for the Thai/Cambodia border area.

Next I went up to the mission to see Peter Jordan about contacts I needed to know when I reached Bangkok, Thailand. Very quickly the pieces fit together. The mission had a young missionary, Joe Harbison and his wife, located in Chaing Mai in northern Thailand. Joe Harbison would come to Bangkok when I arrived.

The next item was to look for the green toolbox. If it were not for the final outcome of this story I would feel too foolish to write this paragraph. For this entire day I was like a robot taking care of one problem at a time. Next I went to the only hardware store in the village and there was a toolbox. It was the right shape but the color was gray. I went back home and told my wife how everything went and casually said that the toolbox was not green but rather gray. In frustration she responded with, "Who cares what color it is, you should take tools." Later I went back for the toolbox and filled it with crude basic tools. As I went out from the influence of fluorescent lighting of the store I found the toolbox was green. Frankly, I don't think I was surprised.

The passion of my call to the refugee camps was so compelling that all else seemed unimportant, like my new coastal cruiser.

My shots were scheduled and I made my reservations to fly from Honolulu to Bangkok on Singapore Airlines. I received a phone call from a Cambodian woman living in Long Beach. She asked if I could try to locate her husband and her family. She was in the exodus of 1975 when the American and Cambodian armies were defeated by the communists. She immediately sent me some flyers with pictures and information about her husband in Cambodia. Very soon I left for the airport with no idea of what would happen next. Jeanne was to follow after a Christmas visit with family.

I had made reservations at the Bangkok Guest House. It was a place frequented by many foreign nationals having their documents renewed. People like missionaries had to renew their visas every year.

It was dark when I arrived in Bangkok. By the time I was in the terminal and at the baggage pick up area, the chaos already started. After all it was Asia. I went through customs quickly and then I was out in the street with my luggage. About ten taxi drivers approached me all at once. I asked how much and got fifteen different prices. I selected the one who knew where the Bangkok Guest House was. The driver drove as though we were just involved in a bank heist. The traffic was heavy and fast. The air was full of exhaust fumes and the strange smells that are uniquely Asia. Tired old buildings lining the rough streets reminded me that this is the 'third world'.

The next morning I went to the International Red Cross and registered with them as a prospective camp worker. In a couple days Joe Harbison came down from Chiang Mai. He had some business to take care of in Bangkok and two days later we flew up to Chiang Mai. It was another chaotic town but on a smaller scale. Here I met Dan Dunham who was a missionary from Texas. He was a very dedicated and ambitious man who had many connections. In a few days the three of us met back in Bangkok. We drove out to the Cambodian border to a town called Aranyaphratet. It was a town of about 3000 people sitting on a highway that went into Cambodia at one time. Only a few weeks before the border crossing had been bombed. The town was a dusty and busy village that had become a favorite spot for supplying black market supplies to the refugees.

The same day we arrived in Aranyaphratet, we met a spokesman for the relief agency I would work for. Joe Harbison rented a house in Aranyaphratet for other people who would be coming from Hawaii.

My first day at the camp was an experience that let me know that there was a major crisis at hand. The main offices of the UNHCR and IRC were located by the front gate, right next to a huge hospital complex. The hospitals, like most structures in the camp, were built from bamboo poles held together with wire and nails. The roof was made from grass thatch with blue plastic for extra protection.

Under the authorization of the IRC, we were assigned to build an emergency feeding center for malnourished children. After that I was assigned to the IRC hospital section to construct additions to existing structures and building new. I had a little spot in a corner of the Adventist hospital complex. I was assigned a group of Cambodian men who worked in exchange for a small allotment of canned food. Interestingly, my green toolbox was on every job. The only problem was that every few days another tool disappeared.

The camp, Khao I Dang, was about 25 miles from Aranyaphratet and five miles from the Cambodian border. The camp was developed out of empty brush land and was fenced as a secure area. Refugees who checked in were literally prisoners of Thailand. This huge area was bulldozed flat and the camp divided into squares with dirt roads. The refugees were documented and allotted a certain spot with a number. An average family was assigned an area fifteen feet square and enough bamboo and thatch to build a shack. The refugees arrived at the camp by walking through the jungle or getting a ride on an IRC truck.

This refugee crisis occurred when the Vietnamese Communists invaded Cambodia and attacked the Pol Pot Khmer Rouge army. As the refugees fled to the Thailand border to escape the war the Khmer Rouge followed and mixed with the civilians for cover. In these border skirmishes thousands of refugees were either injured or killed. Often I could hear gunfire and shelling on the border not far away. Following such fighting, countless trucks arrived at the hospital complex carrying people with terrible injuries and many would be dead on arrival.

The logistics of caring for the huge influx of refugees was staggering. All the water had to be trucked to the camp. It was river water and the refugees had to boil it over small wood fires. The water was rationed at distribution centers. The only electricity was supplied to the hospital complex. Out in the camp, long slit trenches served as latrines and the only privacy was a flimsy bamboo fence. Soon that was pilfered by refugees to improve their huts. Cooking was done in small, dirt pits with wood collected from the scrub forest. This was women's work, and each day they had to go further and further into the forest to gather wood as the camp population increased. Carrying the water in buckets was women's work too.

When I arrived at the camp in the later part of October the population was only about 15,000. When Jeanne and I left in May it was over 100,000. The camp looked more like a place animals should be kept and not people. Absolute basics were given the refugees. A plastic bucket, rubber thongs, a couple pots and blankets and little else. Their food was small dried fish, rice and a green that looked like wilted collard greens. All was rationed. Children who were suffering from malnutrition could go to feeding centers for a hot cereal ration.

By now the refugees had been enslaved by Pol Pot as farm laborers. They suffered from malaria, hook worm, dengue fever, arthritis and malnutrition. All were dressed in rags, a picture of misery and tragedy.

Camp workers came from all over the free world. The greatest number was from Western Europe. The surgery hospitals were operated by the Germans and Swiss. Most of the food supplies came from World Concern and Food for the Hungry.

The human hardships of camp life are something we Americans have little ability to imagine. The smells of humanity crowded in a small place are overpowering. The camp lies in the tropical belt and causes additional problems of diseases like hepatitis and dysentery. Everywhere were unbelievable hordes of flies. Pit toilets were used in the hospital complex and one of my jobs was having my Cambodian workers dig new holes. We would not eat at the camp.

Camp workers understood that their volunteer service was for seven days a week and eight hours a day. One morning after I arrived at work, an IRC truck came in from the border with many badly injured refugees. I watched them unload people with serious injuries and bloodstained clothing being placed on stretchers. It was a frightening sight. One day I watched as they handed down a man to be placed on a stretcher and his arm had been shot off so that it dangled by tissue. It was about now I was wondering what I was doing here.

A couple mornings later I was in my hole at the Adventist hospital when a nurse came in and asked me if there was someone here that could pray for a man who was gravely ill. She said they have a man who was shot in the stomach in border fighting. They had operated a couple days ago but peritonitis had set in and he will possibly die today. She was Swiss. I immediately responded, "Yes, I'll come with you." I followed her to the bamboo ward and she led me to a man lying on a plywood bunk covered with a blanket. No sheets or pillows were available. There were rows of hurting people in the ward.

As I stood next to the young man he was barely awake and it was obvious things were not good. Next to him on a cot was his wife with two small children. The nurse said she was worried about the children. They were dead silent. I tried to imagine what those little brains have had to witness. I asked the nurse if she had a translator. She sent for one, a young Khmer who spoke very good English. I sat down next to the mother near the sick man and reached for his hand. I touched his head and he was very hot. Cambodian tradition is such you never touch an adults head. But now he responded immediately with a tight hand grasp. With the translator I asked him if he was Buddhist and he answered yes. I asked if he thought he might die. Again he responded yes. I asked if he thought that Buddha could help him and he said no. I asked if he had heard of Jesus. He quickly responded yes. This is understandable because there was considerable missionary activity in Cambodia prior to the war.

The translator was very good and drew strong replies from the patient. As simply as I could I explained that Jesus is the only God with power to heal and was as well the only God who can take you home with Him to heaven. I told the young man what he had to do. It was a forceful translator who made the moment full of hope. I felt the woman as she reached to hold my arm. I prayed. I felt there was a crowd around me, it was possible it was not people but rather a host of angels.

The power of the moment was beyond the reserve of my emotions. I only wanted to escape to the outside. As I tried to leave, the Swiss nurse was crying and I said good-bye quickly and left.

At that moment I didn't know where I wanted to be. I could not imagine what could comfort my state of anguish. I knew he was going to die. I only had one choice and that was to go for a long walk out in the camp, far into the camp. The children got used to watching for Caucasians and ran after them calling, "Hello, hello." The little toddlers all went bare bottom because there were no diapers available. As I walked by the huts people would look at me and wave, I would wave back and walked on. The human is tough.

The next morning as I walked down the main road in the hospital complex the Swiss nurse came toward me as she called, "Beel, Beel." With great excitement she said, "He is alive!" She added, "The fever is gone and he is feeling better, he is eating." As I reached his cot he held out his hand for mine with a smile. I sat on the cot with the mother and she reached to hold my arm. There was no translator and there were only smiles and holding hands. A smiling Swiss nurse assured me he will be alright and left to bring the smiling surgeon to meet me. It was a good day for me and them.

It was the first of December and I had not found a place to post the flyers from the Cambodian woman from Long Beach. The IRC had set up an elaborate computerized location system and made no provision for posting boards. As yet they were not receiving inquiries as the refugees were filling the camps so quickly. I had heard that there was a Christian church that had been built next to the Buddhist temple. I decided the next Sunday to take the flyers to the church and see if they could post them.

On that Sunday morning I walked well into the camp to the church. As I was crossing a wide yard area toward the church a young man came out to greet me. He spoke fair English. He said, "Hello, can I help you?" By now there were a couple other young men joining him. The Khmer were very curious people. I pulled out the flyer and there were several heads cramming for a better look. Soon one young man started pointing at the picture and getting very excited. Soon he ran off. The young man who greeted me was Keat. I asked him what all the excitement was about. Keat said that he knows her nephew and went to get him. He asked if I could wait until he gets back.

During the wait I learned that Keat's last name was Khov and that he was here with his wife, mother, grandmother, brother and uncle. They were Chinese. His wife was Cambodian. Keat told me he had carried every one of his family, except his uncle, by bicycle from Cambodia to the camp. All were too sick to walk. Afterward he was so exhausted he slept for days.

Soon the young man came back with the woman's nephew. Everyone was very excited. I got his name and camp number and left him a couple copies of the flyer. I told him to write her immediately and that I would send her a letter too.

Before I left I wrote down Keats camp number and told him where he could find me. The next morning when I arrived at the camp there was a smiling Keat waiting for me. He became my constant companion.

It is a good time to mention that I heard from the woman in Long Beach. She was filing sponsorship papers for her nephew. I heard from her again about two years later. The good news was that her nephew was living with her. But the bad news was that she would never find a single other living relative. Her husband had been executed by Pol Pot.

At the time I met Keat with the flyers, December 1979, there were about 50,000 refugees in this camp and there were at least three other camps on the border. The chances of the woman from Long Beach finding her nephew had to be near impossible. Perhaps I had my reason for being there.

Keat was a wonderful young man to be around. He was extremely bright and serious. Soon I saw him every day and he made a good translator for me. He also gave me a first hand story of what it was to survive under the Pol Pot regime. Pol Pot's terror started when he drove all the people from the cities and made them farm slaves. The intellectuals, business people and professionals were all murdered so they could not threaten his regime.

Keats personal losses were great. He lost his younger brother to dysentery on a Pol Pot farm. Shortly before he and his family escaped to Cambodia, his wife had a baby girl. The infant was suffering from malnutrition and died when they reached the camp. He would have to bury the little girl in the forest in a grave he dug with his hands. At that time he abandoned Buddhism for Christianity. Today Keat, his wife Sok Eng live near us in Kona. He became a very successful contractor. He wisely invested in income property and built rentals that would eventually permit him to retire in 1991 to prepare to be a minister. In 1993 he and his wife with their two sons Kevin and Mark moved to Phnom Penh to start a church. After the church was established they bought property in Cambodia and built a church and home for themselves. His ministry is ongoing. Without question Keat is possibly the most intelligent and determined man I have ever known. He is special.

Jeanne arrived in Bangkok in January of 1980. When she arrived in Aranyaphratet I had moved from the group house and rented a room in a small hotel that was over run with black marketers from Bangkok. It was an interesting game of survival. There are no health laws in Thailand. For nearly eight months I survived on stir fry vegetables and rice, fresh fruit and Pepsi. Jeanne fared a little better on chicken soup and rice. And millions of flies were our daily table guests.

Jeanne had also brought some flyers with her from a family in Ventura that had escaped in 1975. Within a few weeks she had located all of their surviving relatives. She also had a chance to meet the man who had been shot in the stomach as well as his wife and children. Jeanne cared for children of parents who came to the hospital complex for treatment.

Being assigned to the IRC had benefits in many ways. I had access to a vehicle and my association with the Adventist hospital permitted me to have access to medical care. At the time I met Keat most of his family had health problems. His wife, Sok Eng had malaria and hook worm. The Adventists admitted them directly without going through the difficult camp dispensary system where lines would be long. I also had access to the supply list of all the donated emergency supplies that were on the docks in Bangkok as well as the names of the donors. It was interesting to note that the only donors were from the western world. There was not a single donor from Asia except from Japan. They sent a few pallets of paper and pencils. The donors were the U.S., Canada, New Zealand and Western Europe. That was it. At the time I thought that the civilized world constitutes a minority.

Another perk was my access to building materials like bamboo, thatching and roof plastic. One day I was instructed to go into the camp to visit an orphanage of about 40 persons, ages six to twenty. The day I visited the orphanage a young man by the name of Darin came out to greet me. Darin was about 17 and was also of Chinese descent. He was the assistant to an older woman who had brought these orphans together. He was an obvious servant. He could speak

We met Darien in December 1979 in orphanage with Sarin the orphanage leader.

some English and showed me around the crowded group of shacks sitting on a piece of land no more than 70 feet square. After surveying their needs I suggested that we order a truck load of material down and a group of my workers could build a new structure. Darin was quick to insist that he and his friends could build it. At the time I noticed a young man lying on a cot in one of the huts. He was very ill. He appeared to be nearly unconscious. They said he had malaria.

A large truck of material was delivered to the orphanage and I had not heard from Darin again so I assumed every thing went well. One day my supervisor of the IRC said someone wanted to speak to me at the UNHCR office. When I arrived they questioned me about my knowledge of the new orphanage structure that did not comply with camp rules on housing. The gentleman told me that the structure was too high and it also had a cross on top. I told them that they wanted to build it themselves which was permissible under camp rules and that I never saw the finished project. They ordered me to go out there and make them bring it into compliance.

What Darin had done was build a flamboyant showplace that was out of character for the poor camp. About half of the structure was two stories to provide sleeping space for the boys. The rest of the

Some youngsters in the orphanage, Darien in center

Photo taken September 1980 when Darien Chai, age 17, Sok Eng Khov and Keat Khov (both 18) came to live with us in Kona, Hawaii. We met Sok Eng and Keat in November, 1978.

structure was very high and topped with a cross. The older woman was from a Catholic background and was most likely responsible for the cross. The rainy season was soon upon us and considering their small land space I felt the structure should stay. The termites would eat it up in about a year anyway but I told Darin that the cross had to go.

When I was inspecting the new structure I asked about the young man with the malaria. Darin said he was in the loft. I went up to see him and he appeared to be unconscious. I sent a truck to bring him to the hospital. I found out later that he was in critical condition from shock that was caused by his long overdosing on malaria medication. I saw him quite often because he was hospitalized for a long time.

To celebrate the new orphanage the 'madam' invited Jeanne and me for lunch. It was a generous offering and the table was set with some old embroidery work she had carried with her for the past five years. Both Jeanne and I were very impressed with Darin and were led to put in papers for sponsorship. About this time we went back to Bangkok for a rest and to purchase some supplies. We went to the IRC and filed papers for Keat, Sok Eng and Darin. If Keat would get to America he could sponsor the rest of his family.

Keat was having a Bible study where he shared the Gospel with young widows. He had a burden for the great number of widows in the camp and we discussed how we could help. The suggestion of clothing was most important. He helped locate a section where there were widows and children. When we were in Bangkok we went to a wholesale market and bought about eight 200-pound rice sacks full of clothing to distribute. We also purchased about six old-fashioned treadle sewing machines. One ended up in the orphanage. It was quite a job distributing the clothes and would have been impossible without Keat helping us.

In late 1980 Keat, Sok Eng and Darin all arrived in Kona. Later Darin moved back to Washington, D.C. to be with old friends. Four years ago Darin moved back to Kona with his wife Tavi and their three children. As I am typing this journal they are building their dream home only a block from where we live. Darin never lost his flair for big. His new home has seven bedrooms and six baths. We are thankful he is here.

It was late in May we left the refugee camp and Thailand behind to head back to Kona. So many times I questioned why I was there but in the end reasons became evident and this journey became another high-light in my life. We are continually blessed by these three who added to our family in Hawaii.

CHAPTER TWELVE

High Adventure
An African Scam

With the arrival of Darin, Keat and Sok Eng in Kona in late 1980 life became a new adventure. The collision of cultures was always something to laugh about, change and move on. They all shared the same determination, that was to do something with their lives.

My old friend arrhythmia had returned and this time it became a near crisis. My erratic heart beat reached a point where it was routinely monitored with a portable device. There was little that could be done as a pacemaker was not designed to handle this problem. The thing that worked to my favor was that my pulse rate was in the higher numbers, a plus for this condition. At that time the decision was made for me to visit a heart specialist for a final resolution. My first visit to Dr. Lee included another EKG and treadmill run. His remark was, "There is nothing wrong here!" As a second thought he added, "Come back in a couple hours and we will do a treadmill to exhaustion."

My wife and I went to lunch and for a long walk before returning to Dr. Lee's office. After signing a legal agreement, I started running and running. It took awhile until the machine stopped and I was tired. Dr. Lee gathered his information and went to his office. Later we were called in and he told us that there was nothing to suggest a problem. He suggested I quit all medication and precautions and live a normal life. Even though Dr. Lee had no answers I learned very soon that my unexplained recovery made another adventure possible.

Within a couple weeks a refugee organization, headquartered in California, called my wife and me to ask if we were interested in serving as camp managers. The duty would be in a refugee camp in Somalia, East Africa. We would manage a camp that housed a medical team who would care for the refugees. We would first fly to Ventura for instructions and depart for Africa in late April 1981. We eagerly jumped at the chance. Our spontaneous agreement proved to be a great adventure but in the end we found ourselves in the middle of a money scam that overwhelmed us.

When we served in the Khao I Dang refugee camp in Thailand it was obvious that professionals managed this tragedy. The expertise of the UNHCR and IRC functioned admirably. What we found in Africa was completely contrary.

Our first contact was professional and believable. The offer included pay, business class travel and four star accommodations enroute until we reached the camp. Everything was in agreement and the date was set for us to meet them in California. We offered to pay our own way to California and would expect no pay, only expenses.

We met with the organization's founder in Ventura for our instructions. We were to spend three months in a refugee camp on the Juba River that was on the border between Ethiopia and Somalia. Our job was to manage the resident camp for a fifteen-person medical team. The medical team was assigned to give medical care for a designated section in the refugee camp. The organization also had a second camp about ten miles away on the Ethiopian side of the river. The facility was called the Halgen Camp. It was a smaller part of their overall refugee commitment. We started our adventurous junket as we boarded a KLM 747 in Los Angeles and flew overnight to Amsterdam. We traveled in the top deck. It was a splendid place that was never seen by coach travelers like us. We carried with us as luggage several bags containing long-range two-way radios and associated equipment. We were driven to the airport by the founder. He accompanied us through check-in and he seemed to know everyone at the KLM check-in counter. We must have looked important.

We were met at the Amsterdam airport by important people and taken to a fine downtown hotel. The next day we were taken to the organization's office and briefed on their inventory and how to order supplies. This operation was responsible for the supply and delivery to the Somalia camp of every item from food to medical supplies. We were very impressed. It was a very cool April in Amsterdam and the day before we left for Nairobi, a driver picked us up and drove us to the world famous tulip gardens in the country. It was a beautiful sight and we felt it was a thoughtful extra. Later that day we spent a long time walking the streets and waterfront of Amsterdam. It was our first introduction to Western Europe.

The next day we flew again on KLM nonstop to Nairobi, Kenya. When we arrived military guards were everywhere. We were met at the airport and driven to the legendary Thorntree Hotel. It was a large and attractive structure with a huge thorn tree in the front court. Armed guards at the front entrance made the place feel like an armed camp. Soon we were met by a very charismatic gentleman who was the director of Africa operations. His office was in the Thorntree Hotel. He told us our purpose for spending time in Nairobi was to get information about their supply inventory. Also we would be inspecting the new modular housing for our camp. He told us we would be flown by private plane to the mill to review the plans for the housing so the foundations could be started when we reached the camp. Again, we were very impressed with what we had seen so far and satisfied with our decision to take their offer.

That evening we were instructed to proceed to a certain room in the hotel and join the organization staff for dinner. Our personable leader sat at the head of the table and we sat next to him. He told us that prior to taking this job he was a Baptist pastor somewhere in the Midwest. He gave an impressive rundown on the organizations efforts in Africa. He was willing to share everything he knew.

Soon the numbers at the dinner table grew and I was surprised to see that three organization pilots joined us at the table. Our pastor told us that our fleet included two Aero Commander twins and a French-built

The author and Jeanne in April 1981 preparing to fly to a mountain forest lumberyard producing modular housing that never materialized.

high-performance turbo-powered machine. Also they had a couple of four place Cessna aircraft for local service. This organization was starting to look like a wing of 'Air America'. I had the feeling that this was a 'big buck' operation. After dinner we received instructions for the next day.

Our third day in Nairobi was one of high adventure. Early in the morning Jeanne and I were picked up early and driven to the Nairobi airport where we met with our pilot.

The agenda included flying several hundred miles to a forested mountain area where the lumbermill was located. The young pilot told us about our agenda and said we would be flying over a large game park and we would have an interesting day.

When we reached the runway gated area, we were cleared through a group of armed guards before we reached the yellow Cessna. For a couple of retirees this was high adventure and I considered this opportunity a blessing.

The three of us climbed into the flimsy craft and buckled up. The little engine popped into action and we started a long taxi. Nairobi is located on an ancient volcanic plateau at an elevation of over a mile.

We are near the equator and yet the weather is cool, clear and beautiful. I was excited.

When we arrived at the end of the runway it looked miles long. We started our roll and with the three of us and a full tank of fuel the little plane was in no hurry to leave the ground. Very quickly the little engine was at full power and still the plane seemed to be glued to the runway. As the wings tried to grab the thin air there was considerable side to side dancing motion as the wheels reluctantly gave up the runway. It was a struggle.

As we gained altitude we could see for miles in every direction. From horizon to horizon the clear blue skies were spotted with white clouds and the green fields below made me feel like this was an opening scene for a movie. We had to gain some altitude to reach our forest destination. Our two-hour ride took us over a very large game preserve. There were literally hundreds of animals in close view and they all looked like grazing creatures. The terrain was dotted with small round hills like mini volcanoes. Few buildings could be seen. The views of empty green land and mountains seemed endless. The pilot pointed in the distance and said that our destination was in sight. As we approached the field we were still under power. The high altitude made for cautious flying and we were still moving at a good clip for landing. We hit the grass with an indignant thump as though the little craft was saying, "This is enough!"

As we taxied up to a group of shacks there was a truck to meet us. Instructions fell on deafened ears caused by the noise of the straining engine. We were soon on our way to the sawmill in a well-forested area of short trees. I was not surprised to see that the lumber was of a poor quality. The finished lumber resembled something that shipping pallets were made from.

We met the mill manager and went into his office to review the plans. The sketches were the works of a novice and I was concerned how we could make a foundation to fit the modules. We drew some sketches that simplified the location and size of the footings that would be adequate.

We were taken to a shed where the housing sections were being fabricated. Everything smelled of chemicals that were used to control termite infestation. The small amount of work that had been finished would in no way be representative of the information we had received in California. I was sure that we would not see this housing soon if ever. About now my feelings were that of compassion as I observed these men struggling to make a living out of this unproductive forest. Life was hard in Africa. It was a picture we saw again and again. Africa is a continent of struggle and trouble.

Before we left, we were offered coffee. This was a wonderful chance to ask questions about the mill, the forest and what was the market for their lumber. Operating a saw mill in Kenya was not easy and there are no government perks here. It was a cordial time and we wished them well.

When we returned to the plane a very bored pilot was hanging out in the shade of the shack. It was already afternoon and he was anxious to get going. As we boarded the airplane he told us he had to add fuel for the return trip. He quickly warned us that there was no breeze, it was hot and take off wouldn't be easy.

The Cessna had four seats. Jeanne sat in the back and I sat up front with our pilot. His final instructions were that we hold the unlatched doors in a slightly open position during take off. He said it was a safety procedure for high-altitude takeoffs.

As the Cessna tried hard to gain speed on the rough green field there was plenty time for me to think. Things like, I wished the runway was paved, I must be crazy, or what a way to die, on the slopes of a volcano in Africa.

As the end of the field closed in and the wheels were still rattling on the rough ground I was getting concerned. The only indication that the Cessna was flying occurred when the wheels became silent.

As we waddled into the air like a fat goose the first thing I thought about was how these pilots survived the stress. As I glanced at this young American I wondered why he was wasting his time out here. Once we were well clear of the trees the pilot reduced the power and we had a wonderful ride downhill to the big airport. There was a feeling about this place that made me know I was in Africa. My years of curiosity were realized.

The next day was free so we took a walk downtown. We were given strict instructions from the hotel guard about where it would be safe to go. Poverty and misery best describe the plight of the people of Africa. The large number of beggars indicated a very poor economy. A troubling scene was young men, many speaking English, walking the streets and approaching every white person to beg. It was a place of hopelessness. We soon returned to our hotel. Tonight we would eat and sleep in luxury and the hungry people of Nairobi could only hope for a better day tomorrow.

The next day we were taken to Nairobi International airport for our trip to Mogadishu, Somalia. It was to be an easy flight, all downhill to the ocean and only a two-hour trip. From check-in to departure, armed guards were in full view at all times. Relations between Kenya and Somalia were still strained because of the refugee crisis.

Our jet was a vintage Boeing 707 that showed its age. The interior was well-worn. We were traveling on Air Somalia. I had to wonder why a third world country must have its own jet airline service. It is a poor showing of opulence for a nation that can not feed its own people.

The Somalia refugee crisis of the early 1980s was caused by the Somali people intruding into the grazing lands of Ethiopia and Kenya. The entire country of Somalia is a miserably poor place because the land is a barren desert. The once occupying Russians long ago had given up on the country and moved away. The Somalis were a nomadic people whose only wealth was their large families, camels and goats. For centuries they moved about to new pasture lands where ever available.

Their neighbors finally gave the Somali people a mandate to return to your own land or else. These stubborn people resisted and many were killed before they returned home. The forced return of so many people to their poor homeland produced massive refugee camps along the Juba River. It soon became a place of starvation, disease and more misery, and a place we would spend three months.

There was a long delay before we were airborne. As we sat in the stuffy old jet, I was engrossed in reliving the experiences of the past few days. In Amsterdam I felt the organization had a well-functioning organization. But here in Nairobi, I was confused to witness the large number of staff, the impressive fleet of aircraft and the flamboyant flash of cash. With only two small camps and a total of about 20 national camp workers, why is there such a large support facility here? Where is all this money coming from, I had to wonder.

The stress of my worries must have been a sedative because I fell fast asleep. When I awoke the big old jet was quietly cruising at a low altitude over the plains of Africa. At first awakening my first thought was we were in trouble. But this was Africa and low-level sight-seeing with a big jet is acceptable. The crew chose to let their passengers

Author overlooking thte city of Mogadishu, Somalia

enjoy the legendary green countryside of Kenya. It made me wish that every jet flew at this low altitude.

When we reached the sea at very low elevation, we turned north along the coast. After a short time, preparations were made for landing and I was wondering where. The jet made a wide turn out to sea and circled around and appeared to align with an unseen airport or runway. The runway turned out to be a paved strip of the shoreline.

We were traveling fast when we hit the runway and slammed it so hard we were literally launched back into the air. I expected immediate power to be applied for another attempt at landing. But instead for fearful seconds we floated to another huge bang on the runway. There was an immediate scream of reversing jets and the crunching sound of heavy braking. So much for German excellence! They provided the maintenance and flight crews for Air Somalia.

As we taxied back from the edge of near disaster I had a good look at a near barren Mogadishu International Airport. We were about the only plane here. A few low, level shacks were the terminal. There was little else.

We were greeted by some young people with smiling faces. One was a James Dean type and there was also a young woman who took charge of our arrival. She took the responsibility of collecting our luggage. Soon we were in a Toyota Land Cruiser and made our way through a tired city to the headquarters building. Mogadishu was a low, level city of austere concrete buildings. Things looked very poor but there was no appearance that war had struck this place.

Headquarters was a huge concrete two-story structure that was big, but very ordinary. There was a large parking court with at least five other nearly-new vehicles. James Dean just arrived in his like-new black Toyota 4x4 with no top. We went into the large house. The place was in such a state of disorder that it appeared as though someone was just moving in or moving out. Boxes and junk were strewn everywhere. This was no Thorntree Hotel.

In the parking court it was obvious that two of the nearly-new Chevrolet Blazers were not working. And after moving into our assigned room and looking around the big house I was sure this is a dysfunctional organization. I would be proven correct.

It was not long before dinner was served. About ten of us sat down to a dinner of camel spaghetti prepared by a Somali cook. Considering that we were a compassionate Christian refugee organization I was sure that grace would be given. Wrong. We all dug in just like our two little poodles.

Our introduction to the staff in Mogadishu came about by asking questions rather than by well-mannered introductions. Even though we had seen James Dean at the airport he was never introduced to us nor did we know he was the camp manager. James Dean was not only young, but also a thoughtless and indifferent person who lived in his own narrow world. He was about twenty-three. We learned the names and duties of everyone by self-introduction. My first impression of this crowd was all negative. One of the players in the big house was the 'young woman' who met us at the airport and was always seen with a large briefcase. I later learned it was full of Somali currency. There was a middle-aged couple from Holland who were in charge of the big headquarters house. Next was Robert. He was a native of Kenya and a paramedic for the organization. He usually was a designated driver to the remote camp area. There were three young women from the Juba River camp on rest leave. One of them was Rose, the only RN. There were two Somali house servants and several guards. From my perspective of a well-organized person, it was obvious few of the hired camp workers had any responsibility or worked at anything useful. The only productive people were the Somalis.

We spent about four days here before we left for the Juba River camp. There was very little dialogue between James Dean and myself as to what I could expect at the camp. I asked him about the modular housing and he knew little about it. I asked about supplies for the foundations and again, no comment. He suggested I get one of the guards to take me to look for a place that could provide building materials.

We found it was the young woman who was the most knowledgeable about things we should know. She gave Jeanne a supply of cash and information of how to make payroll. She also gave us a supply of malaria medication that we must use during our stay at the camp and told us that Rose would give us a shot to prevent infectious hepatitis. The couple from Holland gave us information of things we could order for the camp and the when we could expect delivery.

One morning five of us loaded up in the big Toyota Land Cruiser and headed for the Juba River camp. Silent Robert was our driver. We headed in a northwesterly direction toward Ethiopia. There was a paved road a few miles beyond the village that would turn into a rutted gravel roadway and finally it was a trail through the desert for 200 miles. We passed through a couple villages along the main road that were very poor. There were a few low cement block structures and houses that were shacks. As we approached the village children ran out to meet us. Some had trinkets for sale, but most were curious. The most pathetic scene was women who came to the roadside to sell camel or goat milk from a clay pot. The milk was dispensed from a single cup.

Soon we were deep in a hostile and faceless desert. Mile upon mile the trail meandered between scrub brush and clumps of low trees, all of which were well-adorned with sharp thorns. The rainy season was just ending and the rutted road was like small lakes in places. Robert was an excellent driver and knew his way. The land was totally devoid of wildlife except for a few hawks that soared above the tree tops. We spotted a few minute deer that were called 'dick dicks'.

We never saw a camp of Somali people but twice we saw them on the move. They moved in groups of about twenty-five people. This included the patriarch and other men, women and children with their camels and goats. At least two camels were burdened with two long poles hung from their backs with the other ends drag-

Somali camel

ging on the ground. At the rear would be a platform that carried possessions and the children. Other camels were led with cargo tied to their backs. The goats were tethered together and led along the trail. Robert told us they were most likely changing pasture grounds. The Somali people are essentially the same ethnic black stock as the Ethiopians. They are of slight stature, tall with fine features as that of Caucasians. Somalia was a Muslim nation.

It was late when we reached the camp. At first glance it looked like a broken-down corral fenced with thorn brush and a few boards. The open area was occupied with several trucks and the grounds covered with weeds and huge clumps of tall grass. Around the perimeter were small native huts made of sticks plastered with mud with a roof of grass and a piece of blue plastic. All the huts had no windows and dirt floors. These small living huts were called a 'modul'.

Our truck had pulled up to the open-air dining pavilion with the table set with plates, face up, and silverware. At first I thought, "How nice, they were waiting for us." How naïve I was. This was a picture of inept camp workers not hospitality.

Jeanne at the door of her office and sleeping quarters, April 1981

Bill at the camp shower

We were the only new residents to the camp on this trip so James Dean's brother showed us to our modul. We would be his replacement. He was about 21 years old with a leather cap and a squeaking monkey on his shoulder. Our modul was the typical stick and mud structure with two cots equipped with mosquito net and frame. The space that was left was for a small desk for the new bookkeeper and a small table for the radio operator.

Of course there was no running water or electricity. Nearby was the shower. It was a 20-foot square structure that also looked like a corral. In the center was a platform with a barrel on top. The barrel was filled every day from the Juba River that passed by our camp. The fast moving water was thick, muddy and filthy. The toilet was an open pit outhouse of unbelievable filth.

We got everything ready for bed because darkness was not far off. Dinner was about to be served and everyone was gathering at the dining pavilion. Already sitting at the table were about six men, all Somali camp workers. I thought this was very strange. The dinner was served without grace and it was spaghetti with camel meat and that was it. A young and tall Somali woman was our cook.

James Dean's brother and monkey were at the table to give us some safety instructions before we retired. First we must wear high shoes at all times and be sure to take our malaria medicine. The big danger was deadly scorpions and camel spiders that measure two inches across. There are snakes and all considered poisonous. It was not a nice safe place for retirees.

At the table were seated, not counting the Somalis, about 14 people. Except for Robert, most were European nationals and a few Americans. There were two people we called doctors, one RN and the rest were nurses aids or simply camp workers. About six were very, very young and immature. My first thought was that this could hardly be called a medical team. Before we left the table James Dean's brother told us he will give us all our instructions tomorrow because the following morning he will be returning to Mogadishu in the Toyota Land Cruiser.

We were dead tired and sleep came easily. The first thing I remember was looking out the door of the modul to a bright sunny morning. As I lay there gathering my senses, all I could hear was buzzing of insects. After I made my way to the outside I found the insects to be flies — millions of them. The open toilet was only 50 feet from either our modul or the dining pavilion. It was not yet time for breakfast and I took a careful walk around the stockade. The only building worth keeping was the medical shed. Everything else was sticks and mud. Every where you looked were abandoned supplies and equipment — all nearly new. There were elaborate water purification units, several gasoline-powered generators and at least six abandoned, petrol-fueled refrigerators. Lying in the grass were hoses, canvas tarps, tents and empty barrels. It was a literal junkyard.

We went to the dining area for breakfast and had an acceptable meal of boxed cereal, canned milk and coffee or tea. James Dean's brother was there with his monkey. He was accompanied by two very young girls that would be returning with him back to Mogadishu. It must have been 9:00 A.M. on a work day and there were very few people at the table. The late comers straggled in as though they were at summer camp.

While at the table James Dean's brother turned the money over to Jeanne. It was a generous supply of Somali money and something I wasn't anxious to be steward of. This was a poor place. Our responsibility was to pay the Somali camp workers once a week. A record of name and payment was all that was needed. The Somali camp workers were the only people under our supervision. All other nationals were paid directly from a bank in Europe and funds transferred to their accounts. Their preassigned jobs were none of our concern. This was unbelievable.

After breakfast James Dean's brother was going to take me around the camp. I was upset and the first thing I wanted to confront him with was the overflowing toilet. First I asked him if this was the only toilet. He answered yes. I asked him if the Somali camp workers have their own toilet. He answered no. I questioned him about the concern for the staff's health and why this mess was permitted to exist. I asked, "You mean the doctors never complained?" When he affirmed that no one complained I was furious. As we walked around the rest of the camp he had no excuses for the total mess and was acting very strangely. I later learned that his parents had been the camp managers until a couple of weeks ago. His father was a retired pastor. This camp in no way represented the work of concerned or even civilized people. The place was a disgrace.

Jeanne had her own burden to carry in the kitchen. The kitchen was a filthy hole with the only opening to the outside a door and small window under the shade of the dining pavilion. Even in daylight it was dark. A single plank platform was the counter. A small gas burner was the stove that was well-encrusted with filth. There was no refrigerator

Jeanne and her Somali helper in the kichen

or fly-free storage area for food, not even the boxed cereal. The dishes were washed in Juba River water and our drinking water was stored in a refillable plastic containers.

The assigned cook was one of the very young girls who would be leaving with James Dean's brother tomorrow. Jeanne soon learned she never cooked or did anything else. The Somali girl took care of the kitchen. Jeanne took over the kitchen immediately. From now on the dishes would be washed in clean water and would not be placed on the table for the flies to crawl over for hours.

While cleaning up the kitchen she discovered huge quantities of canned food from Holland. Canned hams, sausages, meats, tuna and vegetables. When she quizzed the Somali girl about these large unused stores she said it was against their religion to eat this food. Jeanne took over the cooking immediately and camel meat would be served only on occasion. Of course the Somali camp workers were upset.

In only a few hours the relations between James Dean's brother and me were very strained. What I found at this camp did not reflect the work of competent people. However, it was necessary that he drive me out to Halgen Camp. It was about a ten mile trip that took us through a village and over a bridge crossing the Juba River. The bridge was heavily guarded. I wasn't sure if they were guarding the bridge or those who crossed it. Halgen Camp was an area of large trees right along the river. There were no refugee shacks in the immediate area. It must have been protected real estate.

As we drove in the camp there was no fenced area. Just a group of modul shacks strewn about the area. The only structure of merit was a shed with metal roof that covered the water filtration plant. The source of the filtered water was from the Juba River. It was run by two German men separate from our organization and supplied several other organizations. James Dean's brother parked the truck near another corral type structure. This open air pavilion had a thatch and blue plastic roof and was the kitchen and eating area. Four very young girls were sitting at the table and as we entered I said hello and received no response back, this crowd was short on manners. Again a planked counter held a very dirty gas burner stove and empty food cans were scattered everywhere. There was no refrigerator and no cabinets for food storage.

The girls had their own modul. The brother said they were camp workers and gave no specifics. We walked to another modul that had a small shed near it with a pit dug in the ground for working on cars. A man about 40 came out from his modul and I introduced myself. He was from Germany and his job was to maintain the fleet of trucks. Our last stop was the modul of an elderly English doctor.

By now it was near lunch time and all six of these camp workers were doing absolutely nothing. My questions about the purpose of this camp would go unanswered. When I asked why the mechanic was here when all the trucks are at the main camp only was responded with the shrug of shoulders. I could not see a single reason for the existence of Halgen camp.

On the way back to our camp he showed me where the market and bakery were in the village as well as the location of the airport. He also pointed out the World Concern camp as they were the source of the grain meal we used to feed the malnourished. Our conversation had ended until he left.

The next morning James Dean's brother, with his monkey, and the two young girls got in the Toyota Land Cruiser to leave for Mogadishu. The driver was Robert, the paramedic. For the duration of our tenure I never saw Robert work as a paramedic. Before James Dean's brother left he warned me, "Don't make any changes too fast." Later, I would understand that these words were a threat with consequences!

As the big Toyota disappeared in the dust, I stood there and looked around at this decrepit camp staffed mainly with the dysfunctional and untalented. Jeanne and I should have been on that returning Toyota if we would have had good sense.

Jeanne was up early and working in the kitchen and would be in charge of all meals from now on. Near the entrance to our barricade I saw two of the Somali camp workers. I walked over to them and introduced myself. One spoke very good English and he was also in charge of the guards. The other Somali was quite old but a very pleasant man who proved to be a worthy servant. Stealing was a major problem that usually took place during the night hours. I asked where the others were and the guard pointed in the direction of a large modul. I asked if he would take me.

As we entered the modul they were all stretched out on their cots and talking. I introduced myself and asked what their duties were. It seemed they were all 'camp workers at large'. One of them was very young, about 17 and spoke very good English. He was also very lazy. I told all of them to follow me over by the shower and toilet area.

When we gathered by the toilet I asked them who was responsible for the overflowing toilet. No one answered. I tried to shame them into admitting this was an unhealthy and disgusting situation. No response. I told them to dig a new eight foot deep hole, move the toilet and then totally bury the refuse from the existing toilet. When finished they were to dig a new hole for themselves and build a new toilet structure. After that they were to clear all the tall weeds from the compound. These were very unhappy Somali camp workers.

The Somali men are proud and hold fast to absolute male authority. They may not own a single camel, but their authority is expressed by the carrying of a four foot stick where ever they go, usually resting on his shoulder. They can have multiple wives if their budget permits. Everything else is women's work and they are treated as chattel. Building toilets are not their calling.

My next project was to establish camp duties for all the Somali camp workers. Most important was the night time camp duties. We purchased yellow shirts for the guards and they were proud of their new uniforms. Even though there were several, like new, electric generators strewn around the camp there was no electricity for the evening hours. I selected the older Somali to be our 'lamplighter'. Every afternoon he was to gather up all the kerosene wick lamps from all the

Our Somali camp helpers, the 'lamplighter' is center

moduls and kitchen. He was to clean and fill every one and return them. Before the staff had to do this for themselves.

Within a few days after our arrival the medical staff was returning for lunch in a near-new Toyota truck. When they arrived they told me the truck was running hot and making strange noises. A simple inspection revealed the engine was out of oil. Immediately two of the Somali staff had the job of inspecting the fluids and tires of every truck as they returned to camp at night. When I later saw the German mechanic I told him about the truck without oil. He said it was not his responsibility.

The Somali men were complaining about our new menu from the newly reorganized kitchen. It was a problem we had no answer for so we took a drive over to World Concern camp. Their camp manager informed us that we could feed them if we chose but that most camps increased their weekly pay so they could provide their own food. We were cautioned that all Somali camp workers were privileged people who had been selected by the village council. We enjoyed our visit and the important information.

We knew World Concern from Khao I Dang and their credentials in refugee service are beyond question. I was surprised to learn that this refuge camp was not under the control of the UNHCR or IRC. Every organization was functioning on their own at the bidding of the Somalia Government. They warned us to be careful of the spiders and scorpions. One of their workers had been stung by a scorpion and it took a long time for full recovery. World Concern became dependable friends. It was obvious that the Somali camp workers were under some other authority.

The only source of fresh meat was camel or goat. One morning Jeanne asked her Somali helper to buy some camel meat. She told Jeanne that it was not available until a certain day. She said she bought meat near the camp. Out of curiosity I asked the guard where the meat market was. He took me to the main road and pointed to a large shed with a metal roof. He said tomorrow morning there would be camel meat.

The next morning I watched for the opening of the meat market. These operations started with several men walking a large camel to the market grounds near the shed. There was a large flat area of ground that had four large posts embedded in the ground. The camel was led into position and its legs secured to each post. Two long ropes were secured around the camel's neck. Another Somali with a large headdress and wearing a long gray robe was on duty. When the camel was ready the mullah went to the shed and returned with a long knife. I made certain I was a long distance from this ritual.

As the mullah approached the beast, the men pulled the camels head in the proper direction. The mullah made a quick slash at the camel's neck. The poor animal reacted in a furious way that caused the mullah to dance back and forth to make final contact with the camel's throat. It sent chills up my back. At last the camel collapsed in a macabre position partially held up by the poles.

The camel was cut into large pieces right on the ground. The large chunks were taken into the shed where people were already gathering to purchase the meat. The site was swarming with flies at all times. So much refuse and blood had dried into the ground that the flies could only multiply from one butcher day to the next. We were encamped on the fringes of civilization.

In the days that followed I made a point to walk the camp grounds with the head guard to try and identify some of the equipment and supplies, some still in boxes. Almost everything mechanical had something wrong with it and little attempt was made for repair. It was hard to understand that some well-meaning person had donated the money for all this and yet it had little value to this organization. There were several very expensive petrol-fueled refrigerators made in Sweden that were left out in the dirt and rain. It only took a part of a day for us to clean one up and make it work. For the first time in months the staff had cold drinks.

It was still early in our tour of duty and it was difficult to determine the responsibilities of the camp staff. Within the first couple weeks two young men became very ill and returned to Mogadishu. One of them had dysentery. We would never know what their duties were in the camp.

My wife and I were given a small Toyota 4x4 and a driver. We could drive if we wanted but the driver had to be with us to watch the vehicle in our absence. The place was so poor that thievery took place in broad daylight. None of the trucks carried spares. The biggest maintenance problems were repairing flats from the thorns.

A trip to the village market was an experience to remember. Usually a visit to the town market in the third world is to see evidence of an ambitious people who bring the fruits of their labor to sell. Here in Somalia the depths of poverty are so deep there is literally nothing worth buying. The market place is so primitive that everything for sale is on the ground. There is no such a thing as a table. The short supply of produce is placed on burlap bags lying on the ground. Interestingly there was one market product available in great supply and sold by the kilo. It was the grain meal we used to feed the malnourished. It was in large one-hundred-pound bags that were labeled, "A GIFT FROM THE UNITED STATES, NOT TO BE SOLD."

Our only bread supply was an open air bakery with an oven made of river rock and fired by thorn bushes. The bread was baked on tin salvaged from cooking oil cans. The bread when baked was placed on the ground. The village was a place where only the absolutes were available, things like flashlight batteries, matches, and kerosene lamps and wicks. Our big treat item was Coca Cola shipped from Kuwait.

It was hard for me to see any hope for the widespread poverty. I wondered how these people were ever going to take care of themselves in their own desert land. I could not understand why they stayed in this heavily populated filthy place, a place without hope.

Somali refugee children

Possibly this was the day that I became very suspicious of why this organization was here at all. There was no evidence of hope or excitement by the camp staff. I would never hear any of the staff praising any new change or breakthrough in services. They were all simply bodies occupying space for a reason I did not identify with. The fact was all camp workers were paid and their service was contractual. It was simply a job or a paid adventure. We naively volunteered thinking we could make a contribution. The organization on the other hand was there for one purpose, money. We were willing partners of a scam that became more evident by every passing day.

Robert was a phantom that even made the rest of the medical staff asks questions about his strange disappearances at night. One day Robert disappeared for a couple weeks. When he returned he was driving a brand new Toyota Land Cruiser. He had driven it from the French colony of Jabuti on the Horn of Africa. It was a distance of perhaps 800 miles with no roads, only trails through the desert. Rumors were that the new truck belonged to the organization but it was now Roberts's personal transport. Although he had a modul at camp he was seldom there. One day the head guard told me he had a girlfriend in a village south along the Juba River. It was not our problem. However it was obvious this man was part of a broader agreement.

Rose and Sonja, the two RN nurses had become close to Jeanne. All three shared a value system that was at odds with what was happening in our organization. They shared with her the human misery that they lived with every day because of superstition and ignorance. They told her of the primitive practice of curing pain by taking a burning stick and applying it to the area with pain. Then the refugees would come to the dispensary to be treated for infection from the burns. Also there was the barbaric practice of female circumcision. A practice of mutilation of young girls by older women with kitchen knives. It was practice that caused unspeakable pain to young girls and even infection and death. The three became the rock of comfort for the camp, if anybody wanted it.

On one of my morning radio contacts with Mogadishu I asked James Dean what he had heard about the modular housing. "Nothing," was his reply. I suggested that he send a load of concrete blocks and cement to work on the foundations. He agreed and said they would be on the next truck. A week later when the truck arrived we were all disappointed to see that the rough trip had reduced the poor quality cement blocks to dust. Was there anything that would work here, I wondered.

One day when digging in the spoils of the camp I found a very large white tent with screen flaps. I got the Somali workers to help and we built a new kitchen and eating area. We leveled ground and dug a ditch for rain diversion. We took the sand left over from the concrete block sand and made a cement floor for the kitchen. We got a second petrol refrigerator going and now Jeanne was making frozen deserts. The tent became a great place for visiting and hanging out without flies crawling over us.

To encourage our medical staff sometimes we drove out to the single dispensary in the refugee camp. The metal building that once stored the basics for a dispensary had been broken into so often that it became a bare shell. Whatever the staff needed to practice medicine they had to bring with them, even the basics like a chair. Treating a primitive people was not easy. They were suspicious, shy and fearful. There was also a problem with people who looked at the dispensary as an opportunity. That is, they would stand in line and feign illness like malaria, diarrhea or headache. There was no way to prove it was truthful so there was no choice but give the medicine. It was most often sold to someone else. It appeared to me that any efforts of contributions by our organization were more a service of sympathy to a suffering people instead of a healing from darkness.

The after-hour medic was myself. I was to give a package of pills for anyone who came to the camp gate at night. The extent of my practice was to issue pills for malaria, diarrhea or headaches. When called to the gate I carried some of each. It was usually the proud Somali men that came at night for pills. They would be too proud to wait in line at the dispensary with the women and children. I think my assignment gave me a bad attitude. Late one evening a bush taxi brought a very sick man to the gate. As I looked in the back of the truck he was barely alive. The guard told me one of his jealous wives poisoned him. For this case I went for a real doctor.

There was always some sort of crisis that visited our camp on a regular basis. Twice someone tried to take our diesel engine powered water pump than filled our shower tank. It was about the only piece of powered equipment that worked in the camp. The gravity of the latest incident was not just serious but also dangerous. What had occurred

World Concern truck that hauled the grain meal for the starving

was that a large new shipment of grain meal had been taken from the warehouse in the village.

World Concern had been the supplier of large quantities of grain meal that was the only source of fighting malnutrition. They had just delivered a semi-truck loaded with grain meal to the camp. It had been loaded in the warehouse in the village and this morning it had all disappeared. The village councilmen were responsible for the storage.

World Concern instructed that all camp managers attend a meeting that afternoon with the village council. There were about ten nationals at the meeting along with four Somali village councilmen. Two of them spoke English. World Concern was our spokesman. As of now World Concern was only concerned with finding a more secure place to store the grain meal. Foolishly some of us suggested that the grain meal should be distributed to each camp when it arrived from Mogadishu. The four Somali men sat with stone hard faces. The council's spokesman became very quiet. Nobody spoke. In one breath the Somali spokesman said, "It is the job of the village council to store the grain meal." The meeting was over.

It was at this meeting that the first pieces of a scam started to take shape. These were not just village councilmen but war lords. They owned and controlled the refugee camp. The spaces that the organizations were allotted in the camp came with a price. For the refugee organizations it was a platform for which they could promote themselves as a compassionate ministry and collect money on behalf of the poor refugees, lots of money like a fleet of airplanes and wealth. Was worthless Halgen Camp part of the deal? Was it a worthless bragging point?

One Sunday our camp staff was invited to a luncheon at a camp to the south of us along the river. Robert drove us because he was the only one who knew his way through the jungle. When we arrived I was surprised to see how many people were there. All were young, 18 to 24 years, and almost all were European nationals. Camp workers throughout the refugee camps were for field health care at dispensaries only and malnutrition feeding stations. No hospital care was offered. It was a bare bones offering with no overall goals mandated by any higher authority.

The organization that hosted the luncheon was Inter-Church Relief Organization. It was a much appreciated outing but I asked enough questions to know there were very few real medical people in attendance. I also learned that in Western Europe there are businesses that hire people just for these kinds of refugee services. Obviously there is money in the refugee business.

Every morning I cranked up our only generator to call James Dean in Mogadishu. He gave me the big news that Air America would be arriving with their Aero Commander turbo with a load of promotion people. I was to have two of the big Toyota Land Cruisers with drivers ready. They will be calling me at 10:00 A.M. to see if there are clouds covering the mountains. Before long Air America called in and I gave them the all clear and headed for the airport with the trucks. I didn't wait long and a neat Aero Commander touched down in a puff of dust and was soon pulling up to the trucks. A huge crowd piled out. The first to exit was a polished medical team dressed in clinic whites. Two doctors and three nurses. They were as happy as if they had arrived for a party. They were all speaking either Dutch or German. Last to leave were at least two men who unloaded a considerable amount of camera equipment. Soon they were all piling into the two trucks and were on their way. I was totally ignored and had no idea where they were going.

It was too far to walk back to the camp so I thought there could be some interesting conversation with the lone pilot. He was an American and had worked for the organization for a couple of years. The only other information about the organization he would share with me was that this was a TV promotion team from Germany. For the next two hours we just sat in the Aero Commander and talked 'airplane'. The happy actors came back still in a party mood. Soon they were loaded up, the door slammed and in a few hours they would be at the Thorntree Hotel. Right now I wished I were there. There was no doubt in my mind that the demeanor of the pilot suggested he had been told not to talk to me.

This was also the first time I gave thought to the fact that Air America had flights come to the village but there would be no one who came to the staff camp. What was the purpose of their trip?

By now we must have been here about nine weeks and summer was in full hot. There was not a single word about the modular housing. Our minuscule medical team dutifully made their daily treks to the dispensary. If their mission was a calling it lacked all the evidence of challenge and victory. Since our arrival at least three people left with serious illnesses. We would never get so much as a letter from the founder of the organization and James Dean could care less what was happening in our camp.

Things at the camp were so dysfunctional Jeanne and I felt we were simply counting days. Our feelings would soon be realized. The first long count happened one day that the German mechanic said he was ill and wanted to go back to Germany soon. He remained at Halgen Camp and some of the staff thought he possibly had hepatitis. It was a few days later that we received word that the two Germans who managed the water plant at Halgen Camp had come down with hepatitis. We were very concerned because this was our only source of pure water. Every day one of the guards took several empty plastic cans to Halgen Camp to fill them. We all felt threatened and our only doctor could give us little advice.

I had discussed these separate incidents with James Dean by radio and I was disgusted to hear how easily he dismissed a case like hepatitis. He gave no suggestions let alone concern for the victims.

A couple days later we drove over to World Concern camp for some advice about our water supply. The manager told us we have little choice

The infamous Camp Halgen that caused the author's release from duty, April 1981

as this was our only source of clean water. No one knew whether the Germans would leave or whether they would be treated here. I asked what they thought was the cause of the disease in the camps. They said it was always from unsanitary conditions. On this visit I came to understand that they knew there was trouble in the making for us.

It was possibly a week later that we got word that two of the four girls at Halgen Camp now had hepatitis. The next day we drove out to the camp to see the girls. It was midday and all four were just sitting in the kitchen and dining corral. All four looked like caged animals sitting in a dirty shack in the jungle wasting their lives. Why I could not understand. We went to the English doctor's modul and asked him about their condition. He treated the disease like it was a nuisance and told us he was medicating them. I asked the doctor if the girls should come back to the main camp considering that there have now been five cases of hepatitis in this camp. He thought it was a good idea but asked if he could stay here. We agreed and asked the girls to pack and tomorrow come to the main camp.

When I radioed James Dean the next morning that two of the young girls at Halgen now have hepatitis. He showed no more concern than if I had told him they both had colds. Then I added that I talked to the English doctor and asked if the four girls should come to the main camp.

An excited James Dean demanded, "You can't shut down Halgen Camp." I told him the two Germans and the English doctor was still there. He said he would call me in the morning.

By the response of James Dean I knew there was a crisis. I also knew that the phony Halgen Camp was part of the contract with the Somali war lords. Halgen was a token camp that added to the credentials for this organization to exist. This was a dangerous place.

The next morning by two way radio James Dean told me our tour of duty had ended. In two days we would be replaced and we would return to Mogadishu on the big truck. No more Toyota Land Cruiser for us. Jeanne and I were relieved that we would be going home.

In a couple days, in late afternoon, the big truck arrived and James Dean was following in his personal Toyota 4x4 without a top. He would be our replacement. When I went to meet him, a terse and angry James Dean snapped, "Tomorrow you will return on the truck."

The next day we were up early and packed. We had breakfast and met with James Dean for the last time. We turned over the cash box to him and it was finished. All the staff was there to say good-bye. It was a sad moment for Jeanne, Rose and Sonja. The old man, the 'lamplighter' came over to say good-bye. He gave me a big hug and as we parted there were tears in his eyes. Good people can be found everywhere.

It was a long and rough ride back to Mogadishu. When we reached the city we did not go to the headquarter house. Instead we were taken to a very large and impressive two-story house with a fenced court. There were only a couple of Somali guards to meet us. They unloaded our luggage and escorted us into the house. The structure was obviously new and no doubt built for the market of the refugee organizations. We were taken to an oversize room with an oversize bath. It was a place for the rich even though it was sparsely furnished. My first thought was that we were not only alone but we were being intentionally isolated. My second thought was, are we prisoners?

Later the young woman came carrying her brief case and our evening and morning meals. She was very kind and appeared very embarrassed. She sat with us awhile and told us about our departure plans. She told us we were given the best ticket available all the way back to Hawaii. She said when we reached Frankfurt we could change the ticket and reroute it wherever we chose to go. (We later found out it was a very generous ticket.) By now I was paranoid and my first thought was, is this a payoff for silence? Tomorrow evening we would leave on Air Somalia for Cairo, Egypt and on to Frankfurt. She left and said she would bring lunch tomorrow. Somehow the isolation made me feel very guilty. Or was I crazy?

The next morning the young woman arrived with our lunch. It was camel spaghetti and she said she made it. She gave us the time she would pick us up for our evening departure. Before now I had no particular feelings about this woman but now I felt a real compassion for her. I thought of how she could be involved in such a bad situation. As she left, I thanked her.

About lunch time the guard came to our door and told us someone wanted to see us. It was the manager of the World Concern Mogadishu office and his assistant. The two men told us they heard what had happened and that they were not surprised. They said they knew we were leaving tonight, but asked if we would come to their office. We were happy to get out of this barren mansion and have a chance for some conversation.

When we reached the office we were given coffee and something to eat. Our meeting was very cordial. I felt they were picking their words very carefully. And then they asked us if we would like to stay and come to work for them. We would be paid, we could stay as long as we wanted and they would fly us back home to Hawaii. A crest of emotion swept over me and filled my eyes with tears. Their generous offer was vindication and would humble both of us. We thanked them both and told them how much better we felt that someone understood our plight.

I know I mentioned my respect for World Concern as a passionate refugee organization. But how different they are from so many organizations that boldly parade the banner of the Almighty with little intention of representing the meaning of His name.

How foolish we had been. How quickly we aligned ourselves with a corrupt organization. They were a people so dishonest and manipulative they could never share our values. What a waste! What had been our purpose in coming here? Only later were we to know.

About a year later Rose would stop to see us in Hawaii. By the time she left the camp, the modular housing still had not arrived. When

Sonja left the medical team, she returned to the Philippines as a missionary. She is now part of a church, a counseling ministry and still faithful to her calling. We count it a privileged to support her mission.

Within a year of our departure from the refugee camp on the Juba River the founder of our organization was under investigation by the I.R.S. for tax evasion.

It would be several years later that the Somalia Civil War would take place. It would be between the war lords struggling for control of territory. It would intensify, and one day in 1993 America became foolishly involved, causing the loss of American lives, but changing nothing. A movie was made about a failed operation called, 'Black Hawk Down'. To this very day rival gangs control Somalia. It is a place where the poorest of humanity has lived for centuries on the fringes of civilization. And it was a place where I sat with the war lords of the Juba River Refugee Camp.

CHAPTER THIRTEEN
In Life
There is Always a Missing Link

It was the first of September 1981 when we returned from Africa. We had traveled two-thirds of the way around the world only to find we had made a big mistake. This was a journey I would seldom, if ever, talk about. It was only when I wrote chapter twelve that I relived the experience. The ordeal made me feel foolish.

I was 56 years old and found myself at a new crossroad, one that pointed nowhere. The momentum of my past five years had dried up and I had no intention of going back in business. I could imagine feeling like a worn out entertainer looking for a new stage.

The author and his West Wight Potter used to explore the Kona Coast after his African fiasco.

I did not have to wait long for there to be a new distraction in my life, Malaria. I had been infected in Africa. What started as a listless morning by night fall turned into uncontrollable shaking from chills and then a severe fever that had no remedy. Before long excruciating headaches were so devastating I was pushed to near delirium.

In the morning, blood tests were taken and sent to California. The next morning the results were back. I had Malari Malaria, one of the worst. I was also a carrier and was quarantined. It would reoccur two more consecutive years.

It was a slow recovery that left me with little energy or strength. I don't remember making any plans and perhaps it was a time of letting go. After all I was living in one of the most beautiful places on earth, Hawaii, and that should be worth something. After all, during my whole childhood wasn't this place where I wanted to be? I did not have to wait long until I knew; there was a purpose for my being here.

In the listless days of recovery I spotted my little 15' West Wight Potter sailboat hiding under a blue tarp for two years. It had only been in the water a few times on very short trial runs. The next couple weeks I spent great effort getting the little Potter seaworthy with both creature comforts and safety needs. I had a 50-mile shoreline to explore from Captain Cooks monument to the south to Kawaihai Harbor to the north. I got a detailed chart of the coast and started doing some serious boat camping. It was a beautiful and primitive shoreline. It was a place I got to know well in the following years.

When we moved to Kona, Hawaii, it was locked in a cast system. The government was in the hands of a few, the power brokers and the corrupt. The good government jobs went first to those of the right ethnicity. The rest of the Hawaii residents were farm hands and laborers, the rest, entertained, fed and cleaned up after the tourists.... It was obvious, that if Hawaii was not part of the United States, it too would be deep in poverty, misery and corruption just like the rest of the Asia/Pacific nations. When we arrived in 1978, Hawaii was like the southern states, steeped in prejudice. 'Aloha' was only a buzz word.

Kona had always been an emotional place that attracted many of the nation's great achievers, like the men who invented the heart pacemaker and the 'pop top can'. It was a haunt for writers, the movie people and artists. When we first moved to Kona in 1978 there was a pint-sized building boom happening. Many mainland people bought property here only to be disappointed with lack of opportunity and moved away. By 1980 the boom became a bust and Kona quickly became a place of joblessness and misery, especially if you were an outsider.

As I explored the shoreline with my little sailboat I made acquaintances with many of these young people who lived in primitive shoreline camps. Most were surviving on food stamps and picking up any work they could like picking coffee or macadamia nuts. Part-time work in a restaurant was a good job. Perhaps it was my fatherly instinct, but I befriended these hapless young people. I felt led to buy them breakfast, lunch or coffee and simply be a friend and encourager. I could only imagine if it were my two girls in this situation. But I was frustrated at my inability to reach them.

On the Big Island there was an ugly subculture in Kona that comprised the voices of the lazy, the laid back, the hippie, the angry Primo beer crowd and the pot heads. All were living on welfare as an accepted way of life. This 'social hell' was all made possible by President Johnson's 'War on Poverty' that rewarded failure and punished success. An eager Socialist party, the Democrats, handed out these freebies because it made work for the ruling class. (The unionized state and county government employees.)

But there was another movement on the scene that would reach far and wide attempting to gain an audience.... They were the religious zealots. They came with big Bibles, big ideas, new doctrines, university credentials, TV personalities, authors and teachers, all with a new message. They had clever organization names like those of our founding fathers. But they promised new experiences that made the old church sound obsolete. They told us we needed new experiences like: "filled with the spirit" — "we are now spiritual Jews" — "God called me" — "I'm charismatic" — "God gave me a Scripture."

This new crowd brought with them new evidences of faith like: foot washings — slain in the spirit — speaking in tongues — singing in the spirit — anointing — healing.

And soon Kona was on the religious map. We became a haven for specially anointed speakers and lecturers at functions like BBQ's at Stans', breakfast meetings everywhere, love feasts at the Hale Halawai, healing meetings at the Kona Lagoon Longhouse and singing on the streets. Kona became a place where the religious players' petition was, always the same message, "Give us your money so that we can accomplish

'God's Work'." I soon knew that this crowd had a message from 'man' rather than God. I chose to stay away from them.

Apparently my Lord knew my anguish best, because in June 1982 I met a young man in a Kona coffee shop. His name was Phil Mesabaum. He was of Jewish descent and told me he had attended a Christian Jewish Bible camp in 1981. He explained what he had learned and was going back this summer in August. The requirement for attending was that you were Jewish, married to a Jew (that's me) or in Jewish/Christian ministries. The next day Phil brought me an application and within a couple weeks we were accepted. Once again I had my path crossed with someone who would change the rest of my life forever. And I am sure that God knew it could not be just anyone but rather a scholar of tremendous depth of knowledge of the Bible, its past and its future. His name, Arnold Fruchtenbaum. His ministry was called Ariel.

The summer camp was in a forested area of upstate New York near Lake Champlain. There were about 40 in attendance plus children. Lodging and food were included for the three weeks. Except for the information from Phil, we did not know what to expect. It was possible we could make another mistake.

The day before the camp was to start we arrived in Keysville and spent the night in a motel. The next morning we were picked up by a very pleasant but serious man who told us about some of the things we could expect in camp. His voice and words were those that assured us we had come to the right place. By now I had attended several religious camp-like activities that all fit the same profile. That was, a heavy female influence and weak men who had every intention to manipulate your emotional senses. Never once did this happen at Camp Shoshonah.

The first day I knew this place was different. It was a ministry run by men, serious and capable men. They were educated men whose every word stuck to my brain with the glue of truth. The first day we were told that we must read the Bible as a document and believe what it says. There were no emotional testimonies or stories of visions or prophecies or opinions. We were all here for one purpose, to learn.

Arnold Fruchtenbaum was born in Siberia in 1940. He was the grandson of the head rabbi in Warsaw, Poland at the time of Hitler. As the Germans pressed into Poland, his grandfather made his parents flee into Russia to escape death. His parents were sent to Siberia as slaves. Arnold and his sister were born in Russia.

When the war ended, Arnold's family made their way to Germany where they were eventually sponsored by a Christian church in New York.

Young Arnold was curious as to why Gentile Christians would ever sponsor Jews. His curiosity soon caused him to become a Christian. His new faith and hunger for truth eventually led him to study under the top scholars of the Bible. His conservative studies included the noted Dallas Seminary, Moody Bible Institute and the School of Rabbinical Studies in Israel. He soon became a renowned author and lecturer. He is proficient in six languages and he quotes the Bible by memory.

For three weeks I feasted at the table of this man's unmatched knowledge of the Bible For the first time I heard a teacher (rather scholar) of the Bible present this book as a 'Living Document'. It was explained in its historic setting and culture of the Nation of Israel. It was life-changing to know that the Bible was given by God for the ages. Never again would I have to accept frivolous answers for serious Bible questions from those who claim to be 'ordained'.

It was possibly the most important three weeks of my life. The things I learned for the final time were; Except for the first 11 chapters of Genesis and the first three chapters of Revelation the Bible is a Jewish document. It is God's plan for mankind. It must be read in the context of Who – What – Where – Why and When. And if what you read makes sense, look for no other interpretation.

In the Bible, all of God's Covenants were made to the Jews except one, the 'Cursing and the Blessing'. (It is an accounting of how the Gentiles treat the Jews throughout the ages)

The first Jews were Abraham and Sarah. A Jew is in the lineage of a single drop of blood from this pair. To be Jewish is not a religion.

An Arab is the descendant of Abraham and Sarah's Egyptian handmaid Hagar. This disastrous union produced Ishmael. And it would be his descendants that would taunt the Jews to this very day.

Through the lineage of Abraham and Sarah and the descendant patriarchs and their families would come the Jewish Messiah Jesus Christ!

During our last days at camp Mr. Fruchtenbalm had just completed his study on the covenants. The food and fellowship at camp were wonderful, but the accommodations were bare bones. Our little two cot room was adjacent to the boy's bathroom and a good night's sleep was not easy.

One night while trying to find a position that might bring sleep I started dwelling on the only part of the covenant that was to me a Gentile, the 'Cursings and Blessings.' There came a single moment when the cells of my brain reacted as if charged with electricity. Image after image of my life tumbled forth. The images were of Jews who played an important role in my life. First there was my wife who had prayed for me for four years before I finally recognized Him. Then there were those who were my friends, those who changed my life like Al Podell. This very night the faces of all these wonderful people drifted past me like the credit list at the end of a good movie. My life, had been blessed by the 'Abrahamic Covenant'! It was a proclamation from God to Abraham in Genesis chapter 11 and verse 3. "And I will bless those (Gentiles) that bless you (Jews) and I will curse those (Gentiles) that curse you (Jews)". It would be the first time I would learn the significance this covenant had played in my own life!

Camp Shoshanah ushered in a new era for me. From now on I knew Bible truth and was excited about my new knowledge. I was sure my Christian friends in Kona would be interested in what I learned. I soon found they were content with 'experience' and the little 'Jesus stories' about His 'First Coming.' So I began to address those who would listen.

I started hanging out in the coffee shops in the village. Eventually there were those who asked me about the Bible or the Lord. I only answered what they asked and soon there were more serious questions that I had the answers for. Interestingly my first two converts were drug-pushers in the village.

The first was Danny. He was about 30 and was born in Michigan. He told me his grandmother was a Jew. I explained to him why he too is a Jew. This new revelation of his heritage set a fire in this mans' life like few I have known. His brilliant mind came alive to become an excellent witness. The following year he went to Camp Shoshonah. Danny became a serious scholar and a good teacher. But only nine years later the Lord would call Danny home. He was involved in a motorcycle accident. I still miss him.

The second was Wayne. I met him in a donut shop where he worked. He was the same age as Danny but as a drug-pusher he got caught and served three years in a federal prison in Arizona. He was a bitter young man who hated his job. He was a friend of Danny and soon he would try to argue with me about whom he thought God was. It was not easy for him to overcome an unhappy childhood, but one day he made his choice. He made Jesus his Savior and he knew we were family he could count on. He became an excellent carpenter as well as my best friend. After about seven years he wanted to go back to Arizona and mend fences with his family. Tragically he lost his life in an accident. One day I will see them both.

Both Danny and Wayne were hardened young men who had little interest in an emotional dialog about the Lord. After attending Arnold's camp I addressed the Bible as though it was an engineering manual etched in stone. To me it was a 'no-nonsense' document that left little room for argument. I became as bold about its contents as I was about my skill as a builder. I had all the time in the world to share the 'truth' and little time for argument. If someone chose confrontation I would simply asked them if they had read the Bible. I soon earned the name of 'Bible Bill'.

This became the greatest time of my life. Many things happened quickly and with purpose. It would forever set to rest any apprehension whether walking away from my career was the right choice. Or I would not have to wonder how rich I might have been or how great my reputation might have been in Ventura. I would like to share just three incidents that for always will make me say, "I would trade places with no man."

The first incident took place right in Kailua village at one of our most popular coffee shops. I had just finished my morning coffee and was leaving when a young man approached me and introduced himself. His name was David Averre and he was about 25. He asked if he could speak with me. I offered that we sit down and have coffee, but he asked if we could walk through the village. He gave me a short account of his life, that is, he was born in Pennsylvania and was an only child. David was also a child of favor and had an education in music. He was a talented musician and had a job at one of our upscale hotels. David got to the point very quickly, he wanted to know about Jesus. He had all the right questions and was not the least embarrassed about asking them.

As we walked to the town pier and back we had about a half hour discussing serious questions. Soon we were at the parking lot by my pick-up truck. It was a confident David that simply said, "Bill, I want to become a Christian." We prayed together on the spot.

The rest of the story about David was far reaching. The young woman who managed the coffee shop was called Anne. She was a sweet confident woman who had asked me about the Bible but never enough to be serious. But before long it was David who became her friend. Not only was it his witness that prompted her to become a Christian but before long they were married. Their wedding reception was hosted in our home.

Within a year he told me they were moving back to Pennsylvania. David wanted to go to a seminary and become a pastor. He was graduated with credentials for a pastor and education.

The second incident started at the coffee shop. Once again I was leaving and someone called my name. As I stopped a young man called Rob asked if he could talk to me. The conversation took place right on the sidewalk.

Rob was straight forward and very honest. He was an alcoholic and down on his luck. His story was short and blunt. Only 35 and well-educated, he lost everything. A well-paying job as a high school teacher, two marriages and he gave up a young son rather than pay child support. My first thought was I was wasting my time. It was Saturday morning and in one breath I said to him, "Rob, if you don't change, you will most likely die a bum." I added, "Meet me right here tomorrow morning and I will take you to breakfast and afterward we will go to church."

On Sunday morning Rob was there. Over breakfast I told him about the only things important in life. One was to make something of his life. I did not ask Rob if he wanted to be a Christian because he had a hard road ahead of him. I was teaching a men's Bible class and insisted he come.

Today it is eighteen years later. Rob is a very successful man with a very important job and assets for old age. He has his son back and also a granddaughter that is the joy of his life. For thirteen years Rob has been the leader of our Bible study fellowship and I see him every Wednesday evening. He is my friend, a great witness for the Lord and he is my hero.

At this time there was a new call on my life that forever confirmed that I was in Hawaii at the wishes of Another. The years of my life were directed in ways I could never have duplicated or orchestrated. The lives of many young people were changed. For many I would simply be a friend. For some I would shop for land and design their home. For others I would even build the house myself. It was always without charge, but I always told them, they will have to help someone else, sometime.

I could not fully understand my motivation for helping others, however there is an admonition from the Lord Himself, that is. "To those who are given much, much will be required." My bill had come due and I would do my time in Hawaii.

I have lived an unusual life. It was not easy, but it was a challenge. If I am different from most men it is this, I never demanded a high price for my time. But then there is perhaps a reason for this as well. I lived under the shadow of two handicaps that never permitted me to live my life too far ahead. I was born with Arrhythmia, a condition that continually reminded me of my mortality when my heart regularly refused to keep in beat. The other was my affliction with Multiple Sclerosis. I was only twenty-three and in a veteran's hospital when Dr. Brandt told me of the prognosis of the disease. He warned, my life expectancy would only reach my fifties. No doubt, even when I was very young, it was living for that day that made this exciting life possible.

In closing, I would like to share the chronology of a two week budget vacation that was another highlight of this calling on my life.

It was 1985 and the island nation of Fiji was introducing its new airline. An introductory fare of only $300 would take me from Honolulu to Fiji and back. From the time I stepped onto that plane until I returned, my footsteps and words were ordained by Another.

Fiji, like Hawaii, is a destination for people who are searching. In the first week the Lord permitted me to cross paths with seven different people, all alone and all had a problem that they could not solve. None of them I approached, but rather would listen to their problems. With each I could only share what I knew to be true, that is, there is the One who loves each of us and He created us and knows us best, His name, Jesus. Each in their own way shared their burdens and prayed for a new life, the one that counts. It was a wonderful vacation with the days I spent with these people. But soon the final days of my vacation were at hand. I wanted to go into the village of Sigatoka, on the Coral Coast to do some shopping for T-shirts.

The shop I chose had a large selection and was owned by Indian people. The young woman who waited on me wanted to know all about

Hawaii and America. Fiji is a desperately poor, agriculture-based economy. For some reason the discussion came up whether I was a Christian or not. The shop was empty except for us. She asked many questions of what it was to be a Christian. I told her and she prayed with me to accept Jesus. I purchased all my T-shirts from her and we parted with smiles on our faces. I was very surprised how open and receptive to the Gospel she was.

I was strolling casually around the village when a young Indian man came up and introduced himself. He asked if I could follow him to a store near by. My first reaction was fear. I knew these people are zealots for their faith and I was not about to look for trouble. I am sure he spotted my reluctance but assured me it was a friendly visit. When we reached the small store I was introduced to John. He was about 40 and the owner of the store. He told me that he was a pastor of a small Christian church with an Indian congregation. He was most interested in what I had told his niece as she called to tell him she had accepted Jesus. He was very satisfied with my answer and added, "I have been trying to convince her for years she should become a Christian." John informed me that the J.W.'s and Mormons are very active in the Pacific because they promise masked hope without repentance and Salvation.

John and I had a long conversation about our backgrounds and later he asked if I would speak to his congregation at the Sunday morning service. I agreed and asked what I should speak about. He said it is my choice.

Sunday morning John picked me up at the hotel and we traveled for some miles through cane fields to a little inland village. The church was a small structure made of cement blocks with a tin roof and dirt floor. The windows were without glass or screen and the pews were rough planks sitting on cement blocks. The congregation, about 30, sang several hymns in their native language. John spoke first and later it came time to introduce me. He said he would translate for me, line by line.

The message I gave came from the Book of John. In this passage Jesus is questioning believers if they will be bringing other souls with them to heaven or would they arrive there alone. As I described the importance of our witness to others, an anxious Pastor John stepped to the podium and took over. He banged the podium so hard my Bible bounced to the floor. I was fearful I had said something wrong.

I sat down as John finished the service. Afterward he came to me and said, "Bill, it was the best message you could have preached because these people will not witness." As we stood there and made conversation a man came over to us and whispered something to John. He pointed to about 15 people still sitting on the benches. John said, "They want you to pray for them." I asked what for, and he answered that they are all poor and some are very sick. He said his assistant would translate for me.

There have been several times in my life when situations seemed so demanding I wished someone would step forward to help. But today the load was mine. The poverty of this place was so great and these poor souls were so poorly dressed and weary looking I could barely look in their faces. One by one I listened to their petition through the translator and for each of them I prayed. The place was so quiet I felt as though I was all alone. But what I felt was that there was Another who was listening. It was a heavy moment.

The quiet of the place continued until we all left the church and said good-bye. John and I got into his old car and we went to lunch. It was far from luxurious but it was the best vacation I ever had. Was it possible that I was walking with angels?

It is now nearly two decades later and my life has reached into the time called, years of 'great strength', that is, on my next birthday I will be 80 years old. I have lived my childhood dreams of traveling to far away places and realized the gift of many wonderful experiences and have met many wonderful people. I have also come to believe that our natural gifts will never go to waste. To this very day my vivid imagination of interesting structures still permits me to design 'dream-houses' for special people. I have also come to understand that in His Kingdom there is nothing that goes to waste.

In 1977 when I chose to give up my career, there were those who seriously questioned my sanity. But then, they would never know what I gained. How much can be given one man?

Perhaps my story is not unusual at all. But perhaps it is when you understand what an unlikely candidate I am for the missions I have been called to. There are many negatives in my nature that make me a very flawed messenger. I am ashamed to admit it but there are words that define me that I don't like, that is, I am insensitive — impatient — argumentive — unkind — sarcastic — profane and a constant sinner. But somehow, I was chosen to be a player in all these dramas.

Afternote:

In 1984, in Kailua-Kona, I went to see my family doctor. When I went to the counter I was told that Dr. James was not available but I could see his associate. When my time came to see the doctor I was introduced to Dr. Scott Mandel. As a matter of conversation I asked him if he was related to the Mandel family in Grand Forks, North Dakota, the owners of the department store that had the green merchant's wagon. Scott Mandel answered yes, they were his father and uncle. Scott Mandel is still our doctor. It is a small world.

This is also a story about a woman, a companion who was dedicated enough to permit this man to coax her to leave her teenage children in the care of another. And who followed and encouraged him through all the aforementioned adventures. Commitment wears many faces.

In March 1992, I was denied a drivers license because I could not pass the vision test. Over 40 years before the damage caused by M.S. combined with old age would end my ability to drive safely. The bicycle had been one of my hobbies and now it became my means of transportation. That May I took my bicycle to Frankfurt and began a 3,000 mile loop of Western Europe. Since then, I have spent a total of eight summers of solo bicycling in Europe and covered over 9,500 safe miles.

It is now late 2004 and in next June I will be 80 years old. I have made reservations to fly to Europe for the summer with my bicycle for the ninth time. This time my destination will be Tuscany, Italy where I will visit a structure that has always intrigued me, the leaning Tower of Pisa. Obviously handicaps come with compensating benefits.

The author on a bike tour of Europe.

CHAPTER FOURTEEN
A Look Back and Forward

Whether one closes a long letter, or even a journal, the greatest difficulty will be finding words that give the thesis a meaning rather than raw and often boring information. This situation occurred when I presented my journal to Binford & Mort Publishing in November of 2003. As of today, months have passed by while awaiting the long process of printing, leaving enough time for another unsolicited event to transpire in my life. I was soon to turn 79 years of age and about the only plan before me was another bicycle ride in France in June 2004. However, events would open a new challenge for me to which few seniors are ever exposed. After all this is a time for putting my house in order and for enjoying life, hopefully in good health. For me, the demands of preparing for my pending bike trip were the painstaking choices of taking only the bare necessities, much less starting a new project. Instead, a plan was unfolding that I was hardly pursuing much less needing at this time in life. The offer I was about to receive would certainly be the 'frosting' on a life already too rich with gifts of favor and opportunity from Another.

It was about mid-April 2004 when my foster son Gentil told me that there was a man who wanted to meet me. The occasion arose when he was attending an open house party and met Mr. Stewart. As the conversation of the evening was about new homes he told Gentil that he had purchased an oceanfront property and was planning on building. He had already commissioned an architect to prepare some plans that he found not satisfactory. Of course, Gentil was willing to offer up my name, but not without first cautioning him that I was a person of strong opinions and details. The following day I met Mr. Stewart when he came to the job site of a project I was just finishing. This new home belonged to the Chai family. This was our Cambodian son Darien whom we had brought from the refugee camp 25 years ago, and it was a traditional 'Hawaiiana' colonial. As by coincidence, chance or plan it was what Mr. Stewart wanted.

After a short time of sharing building interests, I showed him a couple other colonial projects I had done and then we made a trip to his newly acquired property located just south of Kailua-Kona village in the shadow of the 14,000-foot Mauna Loa volcanic mountain. As we left the main road we traversed a narrow graveled road through a rugged lava field littered with piles of rocks that indicate grave sites left from the Likelike battle grounds of 1819. This bitter conflict came about when then King Kamehameha successfully ended the ancient Kapu system that included human sacrifice. The roadway is part of an old Hawaiian trail that follows the shoreline and cannot be altered from its natural state. It was a slow half-mile drive through a dense jungle that is home to wild goats, chickens and parrots. His lot, one of only seven, is situated in the center of a 500-acre tract of ancient Hawaiian home lands which is a preserve and can never be developed. To describe this property as unique is an understatement. I had hiked past this area many times in the past and knew this place existed but I could hardly believe I would be here looking at property someone wanted to develop for a vacation home. The lot, about one-third acre, was perched about 60 feet above a steep and rocky shore line that is always swept with crashing white waves. While tripping over rocks and brush to get a better perspective of the views and terrain, it was obvious this piece of paradise was special. After a thorough survey of the area and plot maps, Mr. Stewart wanted me to visit an oceanfront home he had rented for his winter vacations for years.

After arriving at the very large and impressive home it was easy to see what Mr. Stewart liked. The rest of the morning was spent discussing what he wanted in his new home and the setting he wanted to achieve. During lunch I sketched ideas that would take advantage of the spectacular view that surrounded this small piece of ancient history. As we parted I told Mr. Stewart I would develop a large scale plan of the lot and plot my ideas of a house design to accommodate his needs as well as preserve the natural setting and view. Mr. Stewart was leaving for Reno the following evening so I told him I would have something the next day.

The following day I called him that my proposed plan was ready for his review. A simple explanation about the design and function was all that was needed to convince him that this was the house he wanted. Mr. Stewart's new dream house would be nearly 6,000 square feet in floor space including over 1,000 square feet in wrap around porches. The large colonial structure graced the natural uphill slope with the forested mountains as background. From the ground level foundation by the private lane to the top of the entry tower capped with a copper cupolo was a lofty 42 feet. The vast interior was soaring, open-beamed space surrounded with traditional columns and folding doors. No glass would block the tropical breeze. Bridging the space between the front porch and the lane was placed a cascading infinity pool that caused the water's surface to blend with the sea on the horizon.

Stewart house at the foot of Mauna Loa

The basic design had taken me about four hours and upon review Mr. Stewart told me to proceed with the preliminary drawings. It was the last day he would be in Kona before going home to Reno. He asked me if I wanted a retainer, I said no. I had spent only a total of about six hours with Mr. Stewart and had known him for only two days and he would trust me with a costly open budget project.

In about three weeks the preliminaries were completed and sent to him for his approval. Immediately he called back and told me to proceed with the final drawings for permits. The plans were ready for engineering before my bicycle trip and once again a set of preliminary sketches would become a new dream house.

After returning from my bike ride in France I had the job of following the plans through the complicated process of obtaining permits on this environmentally sensitive and historically rich piece of land. There was no water, electricity, phone or cable TV to the property. The home would require a $175,000 solar\generator electric system and a 12,000-gallon self-contained water supply using both trucked and rain water. The narrow lane could not permit the passage of a fire truck thereby requiring an elaborate home fire-fighting system using the water from the pool to satisfy insurance company needs.

Mr. Stewart and the author at Lake Tahoe

It was about this time Mr. Stewart called and asked me if I would supervise the construction of his new home. Quite surprised I told him, "I can't drive and haven't done so in thirteen years." His reply, "That's no problem, I'll hire you a driver." It was only a matter of weeks when I was supplied with a stack of checkbooks with my own name and address on them and several copies of his signed power of attorney. The project was a go. No bids, no detailed estimate of cost and only the request for the best job possible.

In the next few months I found that Mr. Stewart was an industrialist whose accomplishments reached far and wide in the 'high-desert country' of the west. His talents reached to farming, electrical power systems and invention. He was a man of great talent and ability. It is only nine months since I began working for him and the huge project is well under way. In the interim my contacts with many of his employees, including his personal secretary of 25 years, Patty, have convinced me that this is not only a very capable man but a very generous and considerate person as well. I treasure his confidence in my talent and ability as the highlight of my life.

It is well into 2005 and the complex project is slowly taking shape by the skilled hands of at least eight men. All of them work with

The author working on-site at the Stewart house

Stewart house under construction

purpose and excitement to see this sturdy structure gazing out to the Pacific. Yes, I too am there every day driven by the excitement of another challenge. I am blessed with the attention of three different drivers who are available to drive me around and help keep the supplies making their way down the ancient Hawaiian trail.

As I write these closing paragraphs I have to brush some tears from my eyes and ponder why this incredible challenge with its opportunity have crossed my path. Somehow the fact of my simple beginning makes it all the more poignant.

If I have just one single closing thought as to why another wonderful blessing has crossed my life, it is this; I have always been a person of great curiosity and enthusiasm. But possibly what was more important is the fact that I could encourage those same traits and gifts in others. The old adage, 'no man is an island unto himself' proves inarguably that we need others to stretch and test our ability and we must learn to give more than we want to take. If there is a single lesson in my journal it is these words from the Master that were penned over 3,500 years ago. "A generous man will prosper." No man can be as generous as He, but my life is a testimony to the fact that it never hurts to try. Is it also possible that it is the generosity of Mr. Stewart that has driven his continued success?

To Mr. Stewart, I want to give special thanks for trusting me with the creation of his new home. It is not simply a challenge of what I could do from past credentials but rather a reason to look at distant hills and wonder what is on the other side. Theoretically, I should be retired. But even at my age my life continues to unfold and amaze me.

CHAPTER FIFTEEN
Vivatson Designed Buildings

From 1970 through 1978, Bill Vivatson designed and built over 90 homes. He designed an additional 30 homes that were built by others, from Malibu, Santa Rosa Valley, Oxnard Shores, Ventura Beach and Keys, Ojai and another 20 plus since his retirement.

Vivatson Residence #1

Tarzana, California
Built by hand by Bill and Jeanne Vivatson
Built 1963

Ventura Keys "Casa Antigua" Apartments

Ventura, California
Five units
Built 1971

Ventura Keys "Casa De Keys" Apartments

Ventura, California
Twelve units
Built 1971

Norins House

Ventura, California
Pierpont Beach, Oceanfront
Designed and built for Dr. & Mrs. Norins
Built 1971

Eckstrom House

Ventura, California
Pierpont Beach
Designed and built for Mr. & Mrs. Richard Eckstrom
Built 1972

Beidebach House

Ventura, California
Peirpont Beach, Oceanfront
Designed and built for Mr. & Mrs. Douglas Beidebach
Built 1972

Sharon Lane

Ventura, California
Pierpont Beach, Oceanfront
Built 1972

235

Vivatson Residence #3

Ventura, California
Pierpont Beach, Oceanfront
Built 1972

Ford House

Ventura, California
Pierpont Beach
Designed and built for Mr. & Mrs. Wally Ford

Vivatson Residence #4

Ventura, California
Pierpont Beach
Designed and built for Bill & Jeanne Vivatson
Built 1972

Maitland House

Ventura, California
Pierpont Beach, Oceanfront
Designed and built for Mr. & Mrs. John Maitland, CEO
    MCA Records, Universal Studios
Built 1973

Channer House

Ventura, California
Pierpont Beach
Designed and built for Dr. & Mrs. Gary Channer

Carlson Duplexes

Ventura, California
Pierpont Beach, Oceanfront
Designed and built for Dr. Carlson

Ventura, California
Pierpont Beach, Oceanfront
Designed and built for a teacher with security concerns
Custom cantilever design

Pierpont Boulevard

Ventura, California
Pierpont Beach

Vivatson "Spec" House

Ventura, California
Pierpont Beach

Vivatson Duplexes

Ventura, California
Pierpont Beach
Designed and built for Bill & Jeanne Vivatson

Vivatson Triplex

Ventura, California
Pierpont Beach
Designed and built for Bill & Jeanne Vivatson

Pierpont Bay Realty

Ventura, California
Pierpont Beach
Received an award for "Remodel of the Year"
Remodeled from a single story hamburger stand to a two-story
Tudor realty and engineers office building.

Lavery House

Ventura, California
Ventura Keys Waterfront
Designed and built for Mr. & Mrs. Lavery
Built 1975

Vivatson Residence #2

Ventura, California
Ventura Keys, Waterfront
Designed and built for Bill & Jeanne Vivatson

Sakaroff House

Ventura, California
Ventura Keys, Waterfront
Designed and built for Mr. & Mrs. Al Sakaroff
Built 1977

Montague House

Ventura, California
Ventura Keys
Designed and built for Dr. & Mrs. Montague

Flanigan House

Oakview, California
Designed and built for Mr. & Mrs. Flanigan
Built 1977

Nielson House

Ojai, California
Designed and built for Mr. & Mrs. Nielson
Built 1977

253

Casitas Lake View House

Ojai, California
Designed and built for Wally & Connie Ford
Built 1977

Saddle Mountain House

Ojai, California
7,000 sq. ft.
Built 1976

Leonard Residence

Oakview, California
Rancho Matilija, 8,000 sq. ft. with pool and spa
Designed and built for Dr. & Mrs. Leonard

256

Saticoy Residence

Saticoy, California
Custom home with specially designed garage for client's sail plane

Gallion Residence

Santa Ynez, California
Five acre horse ranch in Santa Barbara County

Vivatson Kona House

Kona, Hawaii
Designed and built for Bill & Jeanne Vivatson
Built 1979

Vivatson Rental

Kona, Hawaii
Rental Property
Designed and built for Bill & Jeanne Vivatson

Vivatson Rental

Kona, Hawaii
Rental Property
Designed and built for Laura Vivatson

Chai Residence

Kona, Hawaii
Designed and built for Mr. & Mrs. Darien Chai

Leonard Vacation Guest House

Kahalu'u, Hawaii
Designed and built for Dr. & Mrs. Leonard

Stewart House

Kailua-Kona, Hawaii
Designed and built for Mr. Mike Stewart
5,000 sq. ft.
Under construction 2006

Stewart River Cabin

Proposed plan 2005
North Fork of Clear River Canyon, Idaho
Proposed Riverside 20 unit Condominium Project
Designed for Mr. Mike Stewart
First model under construction 2006